Coastal Knits

A Collaboration between Friends on Opposite Shores

by **ALANA DAKOS** OF NEVER NOT KNITTING and **HANNAH FETTIG** OF KNITBOT

THIRD EDITION v.092712

A special thanks to **my husband, Jason, and the rest of my family** for always being there for me. Thank you too to all of my blog readers and podcast listeners for all of their support and for the motivation they have given me in continuing on in my design work.

My share of *Coastal Knits* is dedicated to **my father, Scott**, who instilled a love of nature in me at an early age and who introduced me to the wonderful local regions that are featured in this book.

For **Abe, Jonah and Mabel**, thanks for supporting my love for knitting. I love our happy home!

Also, thanks to **my grandmother, June Smith**, for teaching me how wonderful handcrafting can be. You're right, it is.

To those who continue to knit my patterns, thank you. I love my job!

Alana

Hannah

Photographs copyright ©2012 Hannah Fettig and Alana Dakos, except where noted
Photographs copyright ©2012 Carrie Bostick Hoge (pages 4–5, 12–13, 21–25, 34–39, 48–55, 62–67, 74–79, 87)
Illustrations copyright ©2012 Neesha Hudson

ISBN (e-book) 978-0-615-69655-3
ISBN (printed book) 978-0-615-52934-9
Library of Congress Control Number: 2012917288

Third edition; printed in China
Published by Dakos and Fettig Publications / PO Box 1635 / Atascadero, CA 93423

Technical editing by Tana Pageler, Cecily Glowik MacDonald and Kristen TenDyke
Graphic design by Mary Joy Gumayagay

Wildflower Cardigan 40

Sand and Sea
Shawlette 80

Panoramic Stole 62

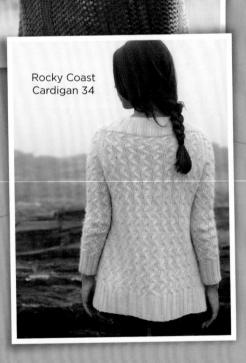

Rocky Coast
Cardigan 34

Gnarled Oak Cardigan 26

Water's Edge Cardigan 48

Branching Out Mitts 74

Cambrian Cowl 68

Rustling Leaves Beret 56

Bayside Pullover 20

Monogram watermarks indicate whether a design was created by Alana or Hannah

Once upon a time we met online after being introduced by a mutual friend. Instantly we realized that we had quite a bit in common and started communicating regularly. We were able to finally meet in person when Hannah's tour for her first book brought her and her husband to California, and our families got to spend a few days together at Alana's home. Although we lived on opposite ends of the country, we were pleasantly surprised by how many similar interests our families shared. Spending the weekend together felt like spending time with old friends rather than new ones, as if we had known each other for many years.

Over the years that followed we kept in contact as our families and pattern lines grew, and we frequently asked one another for advice and input. Our design styles differ, yet we have an

COASTAL KNITS

appreciation for each other's work and have enjoyed knitting each other's patterns.

We each toyed with the idea of self-publishing books, but being busy, work-at-home moms made it seem a daunting task. After much discussion, we decided that a collaborative design project could make this more of a possibility. It certainly would be fun and interesting! Quickly the concept for *Coastal Knits* began to take shape, and we were instantly full of ideas and excitement for this project. We wanted *Coastal Knits* to be a merging of not only our opposite shorelines, but also of our two personalities and backgrounds.

As an East Coast native, Hannah designs classic sweaters for a modern audience. Her Knitbot pattern line is known for wearable and stylish sweaters, the most popular being her *Featherweight Cardigan*. Alana, a West Coast native, is drawn to romantic styling, feminine details, and intricate stitches. She draws most of her inspiration from the natural world around her and enjoys working botanical design elements into her stitch patterns.

Although our design aesthetics differ, we feel that our individual work complements each other nicely. You will find a little piece of each of us in *Coastal Knits*.

A COLLABORATION BETWEEN FRIENDS ON OPPOSITE SHORES

We feel privileged to have grown up in two very beautiful coastal regions that have not only shaped our design work, but also who we are as individuals. Each design featured in *Coastal Knits* has been inspired by one of our favorite local locations. Before each pattern you will find an inspiration board featuring photographs along with an essay on what makes this particular destination special to us personally.

We have enjoyed working together to bring *Coastal Knits* to you. We hope it brings you hours of contented knitting and that it motivates you to find inspiration in your own surroundings.

Alana   *Hannah*

NAME *Alana Dakos, aka*

Never Not Knitting

HOMETOWN *Atascadero, California*

BEST KNOWN FOR *Hosting the Never Not Knitting podcast and designing patterns such as the Cedar Leaf Shawlette and Shawl Collared Cowl.*

FAVORITE COLORS *Green, brown, orange, red and gold*

HOW DID YOU GET STARTED WITH KNITTING? *I taught myself to knit and crochet shortly after I was married in 2002. It was love at first stitch! A year or so later I signed up to teach knitting and crochet classes at different places in my local community, and started selling scarves and hats of my own design at different events in the area. Before long I was working at my local yarn shop and teaching several knitting classes per week. In the summer of 2008 I launched the Never Not Knitting podcast, a biweekly knitting show featuring yarn reviews, knitting stories and designer interviews. In 2009, I decided to branch out further and try my hand at knitwear design. That decision led to the beginnings of our now full-time, family pattern business. Knitting will always be my passion. I don't like to go a day without getting even just a little knitting time in.*

WHAT INSPIRES YOU? The natural world around me. I often draw my design inspiration from plants, leaves and trees.

WHAT DO YOU LOVE ABOUT CALIFORNIA? The mild coastal climate, the diverse and beautiful scenery, and the friendly people in my community.

WHAT ARE YOUR FAVORITE PLACES?

Montaña De Oro: A unique, local state park with eucalyptus groves, sandy trails and magnificent tide pools. I've spent many outings there over the years. It's such a peaceful place.

Moonstone Beach Boardwalk: This is one of my favorite places to walk with my family. We completed this trail several times with my then-baby daughter in her stroller. It holds many memories for us.

Morro Strand Beach: A lovely little stretch of beach in Morro Bay. Morro Bay is our favorite spot to eat fish and chips by the ocean.

Oaks State Reserve: An eerie, ancient forest of Oak trees, gnarled and bent with age. I have fond childhood memories of going here with my dad and brother.

Shell Creek Road: A hidden local spot known for its spectacular wild-flowers. I look forward to picnicking there every year with my family and all my friends.

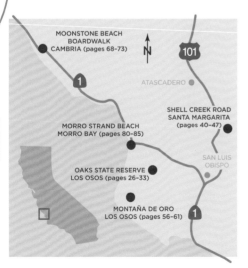

MOONSTONE BEACH
BOARDWALK
CAMBRIA (pages 68–73)

101

ATASCADERO

SHELL CREEK ROAD
SANTA MARGARITA
(pages 40–47)

MORRO STRAND BEACH
MORRO BAY (pages 80–85)

SAN LUIS
OBISPO

OAKS STATE RESERVE
LOS OSOS (pages 26–33)

MONTAÑA DE ORO
LOS OSOS (pages 56–61)

Trained originally as a printmaker, Krista McCurdy began applying the color sense she developed to yarn and fiber when she started her company, **Pigeonroof Studios,** *in 2007. Living in the temperate yet rather unpredictable climate of the San Francisco Bay Area, Krista has been inspired to choose yarns and create colorways that reflect the year-round climate and color surrounding her. The greens of local plants, the blues of the ocean and the smokey greys of the fog keep her constantly fueled with inspiration. Even in the height of summer, the fog rolling off of the Pacific can make wearing wool a necessity, so Krista has incorporated many different fiber options into her line. Pigeonroof Studio yarns are wonderfully saturated, sophisticated and extremely luxurious. It was an obvious choice for me to use in Coastal Knits and I enjoyed working every stitch of this amazing yarn. pigeonroofstudios.etsy.com / pigeonroofknits.blogspot.com*

When Tactile Fiber Arts *agreed to create a special natural-dyed yarn for Coastal Knits, I was thrilled! I love working with her yarns and I love the story behind her company. Maia Discoe started Tactile in 2007 out of a love for wool. Tactile specializes in naturally-colored yarns and fibers dyed in earth-friendly vibrant hues. The dyes used are all from nature: leaves, bark, roots, flowers, and even insects. They are all from sustainable sources and usually organically grown while remaining fade resistant and wash fast.*

Her new Wild Crafted *series uses plant materials gathered in her local region of California such as eucalyptus leaves and bark, plum leaves, and horsetail. Tactile colorways are inspired by and named after nature. Her favorite influences are the briny smell of the Pacific Ocean air, the soft and complex colors created by the coastal fog, the colors and textures of the tidal marshes, and the trees shaped by the wind. Located on the temperate California Coast, Maia is able to work outside all year: never too hot, never too cold. Her employees are Sammie, the Boston terrier in charge of keeping the squirrels at bay, and the afternoon ocean breeze to dry the yarns. www.tactilefiberarts.com*

california yarns

Alpenglow Yarn *is a small hand-dyed yarn company based in the Central Coast of California. Former engineer Carrie Sundra adventurously started Alpenglow in 2009 in order to pursue a life of color, leaving behind her former gray cubicle career. This small local company focuses on supporting American farming while using natural dye techniques. Her* Small Farm Yarn *line is sourced directly from local farms by Carrie herself and much is processed at a local family-run mill,* Ranch of the Oaks. *The alpaca yarns can be traced back to the specific contributing alpacas whose names grace each yarn label. Carrie loves living in the Central Coast as much as I do and draws inspiration for her work from the character of our local community, as well as the rolling hills of the California landscape. Working with Alpenglow Yarn, I felt a strong connection to the beautiful area which we call home. www.alpenglowyarn.com*

NAME Hannah Fettig, aka

knitbot

HOMETOWN Portland, Maine

BEST KNOWN FOR Featherweight, Whisper and Effortless Cardigans

FAVORITE COLORS Grey and yellow

HOW DID YOU GET STARTED WITH KNITTING?
I learned to knit from my grandmother when I was young. I always fiddled with it, but I fell in love when a cool local yarn shop opened in my area. I couldn't stay away! Soon I was working there, and I always say this "fast forwarded" my knitting experience, as I was fully immersed in it.

I tried my hand at designing a few things. My first real opportunity was for The Fibre Company, which had started their mill right down the street from the shop I was working at. While attending a trade show with them, I met a craft book editor and landed myself a book deal. My real success, however, came after the release of my Whisper Cardigan pattern in the spring 2009 issue of Interweave Knits. This was a jumping-off point for my self-published line of Knitbot patterns.

I've established my niche designing simple, classic sweaters for today's modern woman.

String Theory Hand Dyed Yarn *is a small yarn company located in a historic house on the peninsula of Blue Hill, Maine. Blue Hill is home to many artists and creative folk, and it's no wonder. There is a raw, natural beauty to the rugged rocky shores that ring the islands and inlets. Everywhere you look there is color: the rich greens and browns of the forests, fields and rocks that gain intensity when it's foggy. At the water's edge there are gray-green lichens on the pink granite and the endless blues of the sea and sky. It is evident from the rich color palette of String Theory Hand Dyed Yarns that dyers Tanis Williams and Karen Grover are inspired by the beauty that surrounds them.*

Tanis and Karen met when they were labor and delivery nurses working in the same small local hospital. They quickly discovered a common love of knitting, fabric and colors. They started dyeing together and soon had more on their hands than they could ever knit themselves. After an overwhelming reception from a local yarn shop that started carrying their yarns, they gained the confidence that other people valued what they were doing. They started dyeing yarn seriously and Karen and her husband bought an old house in Blue Hill. In 2006, after 8 months of restoration on the historic house, String Theory Hand Dyed Yarn had a home of its own. Initially they carried more commercial yarn, but over the years, the yarns they dyed on more than a dozen different bases occupied most of the room at the shop. With such a direct connection between the Maine coast and String Theory Hand Dyed Yarn, it was a perfect choice for my Coastal Knits *collection. www.stringtheoryyarn.com*

maine yarns

Situated off the Maine coast, **Swans Island**, headquartered in Northport, is like visiting somebody's home. The entire company, including manufacturing—if you can call hand-dyeing and hand-weaving manufacturing—is housed in a weathered 1780s cape that overlooks Maine's Penobscot Bay.

Twenty years ago, John and Carolyn Grace moved to Swans Island with a passion for the place and an idea: to make blankets from the wool of hardy island sheep, blankets that were spare and elegant and timeless. In 2003 they retired, and new owners took over their venture, the whole thing: blankets, ideals and passion. They moved it close to their own homes on the Midcoast. The business seems like a family enterprise: everybody—from the weavers to the designers—lives nearby. It is a community. The house is literally a cottage industry.

The company now makes yarn for hand knitting in three weights and an array of rich colors. Certified 100% organic, it is spun at a historic Maine mill that has been making yarn for over 100 years, and dyed with all-natural dyes at the 1780s cape in Northport. Less processing makes the finished yarn incredibly soft. Once I discovered this I knew I needed to include Swans Island yarn in my Coastal Knits collection. It is inspired by and made right here in Maine. What a gift to the knitting community! www.swansislandblankets.com

My most popular patterns are the ones that use lace or fingering weight yarn knit at a looser gauge. It creates a fabric that hangs like jersey—so comfortable!

WHAT INSPIRES YOU? I'm inspired by current and vintage fashion, my city, the ocean, and the change in seasons.

WHAT DO YOU LOVE ABOUT MAINE? I love the hard-working people of Maine, the beauty that surrounds us here on the coast, and the diversity that comes from having four real seasons.

WHAT ARE YOUR FAVORITE PLACES?
Casco Bay: I live by the bay. Breathing ocean air every day is such a privilege.

Eastern Promenade: This park wraps around the wonderful Munjoy Hill neighborhood, where I fell in love with knitting. There are beautiful, panoramic views from great heights.

The West End: I called this quiet Portland neighborhood home for many years. Its wide, tree-lined streets are lovely to stroll and feature amazing architecture.

Two Lights State Park: This is the rocky Maine Coast at its best! There are shelves upon shelves of rocks to explore as the waves of the Atlantic ocean crash down.

Willard Beach: This is my favorite walking beach. My memories of it surround meeting my husband. Now, as a family, we spend a lot of time there.

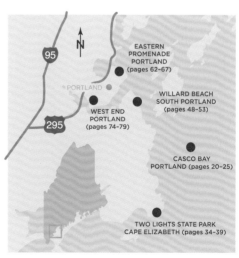

Check. Your. Gauge.

"Any good knitting book will tell you to do this, and with good reason! You might hesitate to take the extra time, but think of all the time you're going to invest in knitting an entire project. Do you want to take the of risk of it coming out too small or too large?" - Hannah

"Take it from me, gauge is the most crucial step in planning a project. I've knit way too many ill-fitting sweaters in my day and have learned this lesson the hard way. Just a little bit of difference in a gauge swatch can mean inches of difference in your finished garment. Unless you are a risk taker who doesn't mind gambling with the outcome of a skin-tight or too-baggy sweater, this is a step not to be overlooked." - Alana

HOW TO CALCULATE GAUGE: For each project, gauge is given for a 4" / 10cm square. This sample square is used to measure your stitches and make sure that your finished garment will turn out the correct size.

> *Example gauge: 24 sts and 30 rows = 4" / 10cm in St st on US6 / 4mm needles or size needed to obtain gauge.*

Start with a US6 / 4mm needle and cast on 24 stitches. Work in Stockinette stitch for 30 rows and bind off. Block your swatch (see *The finishing touches* on the next page). If your swatch measures 4" / 10cm on each side, you are good to go! If your swatch measures too small, go up a needle size and try again. If your swatch measures too large, it's time to go down a needle size. Knit a new swatch, block and remeasure. Whichever needle size

gives you the correct gauge is the size you will use for your project.

Trust us, it's worth the time to check gauge!

Choose your yarn carefully

Would you like to substitute a yarn from your stash or that new tempting yarn from your LYS instead of the yarn we used for a project? No problem! In each pattern we've provided you with some alternative yarn suggestions to make the transition easier. But what if you have another yarn in mind?

YARN WEIGHT AND GAUGE: These are the first things to consider when substituting. If a pattern calls for a worsted weight yarn, substitute with a yarn of the same weight.

FIBER CONTENT: Because of the nature of the fiber used (such as merino, alpaca, linen), some yarns have more drape while others offer better stitch definition, etc.

Yarns used in the designs from the book were chosen for a reason. Keep in mind the properties of the original yarn when making a substitution. Once you find a comparable yarn that you like, it's time to swatch! Try using a few different needle sizes to see if you can match the project gauge exactly.

Get familiar with the instructions

It's always a good idea to read through a pattern before you begin. This gives you the full scope of the pattern and allows you to get a feel for how the item is constructed. It would also be helpful for you to make sure that you have all of the tools you need before you start, and to see if there are any instructions that you may need help in understanding. If you come across an instruction or abbreviation that you are not familiar with, see Techniques and Abbreviations on pages 88–89.

When choosing the appropriate garment size, take a careful look at the schematic provided. Compare your body measurements against the garment's, keeping in mind the recommended ease, and pick the size that will offer the most flattering fit. You can always make simple adjustments such as adding a few inches to the body or sleeve length if necessary.

Charts and how to read them

You might stumble upon funny little boxes containing hieroglyphics. These are charts and many knitters use them. But don't worry, if you are not the chart loving type, written instructions have also been provided for most patterns.

If you choose to work from the chart, keep in mind that all charts start at the bottom and read from right to left on right side (RS) rows, and left to right on wrong side (WS) rows. If a chart is repeated, it's helpful to place markers between repeats until the pattern is established.

"I find it quite helpful to start out with the written instructions until I get a feel for the stitch pattern. After I'm comfortable working the stitches, I can then switch over to the chart with ease." - Alana

The finishing touches

Blocking is an important final step for even the smallest of projects. Blocking evens out wayward stitches and provides your garment with added drape and a neat, polished look. Even the most beautiful knitted item hasn't reached its full potential until it's had a good blocking.

Refer to the schematic for the specific finished measurements for each part of your project. There are a few different methods that knitters use, but we both prefer to wet block.

"I fill my washing machine with enough cold water to immerse my project, adding in some wool wash if desired. I let the project soak for 10 minutes and then run the spin cycle. I then gently squeeze out as much water as I can, then roll it up in a big towel to get even more water out. I usually lay my piece flat on a carpet, bedspread or blocking board. Following the schematic, I stretch my piece into shape, using blocking pins to hold it down, allowing it to dry completely, around 24 hours." - Hannah

"I block my handknits in the bathroom sink or in a large kitchen bowl with lukewarm water and a wool wash such as Eucalan or Soak. If I'm blocking something knit from wool, I am careful not to agitate the item too much or use water too hot for fear of felting it. After soaking it for several minutes, I squeeze out as much water as possible, roll up the handknit in a large towel and get my 5-year old daughter to step all over it to get out all of the excess water. (Her most favorite activity!) I then lay it out on my dining room table covered with bath towels and stretch the item to the correct measurements. I choose my table because not only is it a large flat surface, but it's off of the floor, out of the way and under a ceiling fan. The fan cuts the drying time in half!" - Alana

Last but not least...

Preparing well before starting a project will help ensure that the finished item turns out exactly the way you hoped it would. We hope that you enjoy knitting our *Coastal Knits* patterns and that these knits will be wardrobe staples for years to come.

HAVE A QUESTION ABOUT A PATTERN?
Email technicalsupport@coastalknits.com

PATTERN CORRECTIONS
Visit www.coastalknits.com/errata

JOIN THE COASTAL KNITS *RAVELRY* GROUP!
Share all your *Coastal Knits* project photos and experiences with other knitters at www.ravelry.com/groups/coastal-knits

We can't wait to see your finished projects!

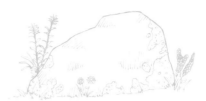

SWEATERS

Casco Bay

One of the things that makes Portland, Maine so special is Casco Bay. Downtown Portland is on a hill, and as I walk through town, crossing streets that slope down toward the water, I catch glimpses of the harbor between brick buildings. The bay is an estuary, a place where fresh- and saltwater meet, and it's saltier than most. Locals say it's a perfect environment for lobsters, which Maine is known for. Teeming with marine life, the bay is also home to many species of waterbirds which I always see soaring in the sky above town. Casco Bay is both a working waterfront for oil tankers and bulk cargo transports, and a port of call for cruise ships. Visitors come to tour the many islands, historic forts, and lighthouses found here.

The **Bayside Pullover** is inspired by this waterfront, with a rope-like cable that runs along the raglan seams and continues down the sides. Knit in organic linen, it evokes the nets and traps used by the fisherman in these waters.

I see Casco Bay, everyday. It's a significant part of my life, literally surrounding me. This contributes to my sense of place in the world: I live by the bay. I feel fortunate to be able to say that and I'm content to imagine being here for years to come.

A working waterfront and a scenic playground for locals and tourists.

I needed a yarn that would make the cables feel like rope.

This organic linen was perfect. Also, it's very comfortable to knit and wear.

bayside pullover

This breezy raglan pullover is worked from the top down in the round. A simple cable follows the raglan lines and continues down the sweater sides. The original is worked in linen, making it great for warmer climates. For a pullover to wear in cooler weather, work it in a fingering weight wool.

Yoke

With shorter circular needle, CO 72 (74, 76, 72, 74, 76, 72, 74) sts.

Setup row (WS): P1 right front st, pm, k2, p6, k2, pm, p6 (6, 6, 4, 4, 4, 2, 2) sleeve sts, pm, k2, p6, k2, pm, p18 (20, 22, 22, 24, 26, 26, 28) back sts, pm, k2, p6, k2, pm, p6 (6, 6, 4, 4, 4, 2, 2) sleeve sts, pm, k2, p6, k2, pm, p1 left front st.

RAGLAN INCREASE AND NECK SHAPING

Row 1 (RS): {Knit to marker, M1R, sm, work Bayside Cable patt over next 10 sts, sm, M1L} 4 times total. Knit to end. Using backward loop method, CO 2 sts.

Row 2 (WS): {Purl to marker, sm, work Bayside Cable patt over next 10 sts, sm} 4 times total. Purl to end. Using backward loop method, CO 2 sts. 12 sts inc.

Rep last 2 rows 2 [2, 3, 3, 3, 4, 4, 4] times more. 108 (110, 124, 120, 122, 136, 132, 134) sts total: 10 (10, 13, 13, 13, 16, 16, 16) sts for each front, 10 sts for each cable, 12 (12, 14, 12, 12, 14, 12, 12) sts for each sleeve, 24 (26, 30, 30, 32, 36, 36, 38) back sts.

Next row (RS): {Knit to marker, M1R, sm, work Bayside Cable patt over next 10 sts, sm, M1L} 4 times total. Knit to end. Using backward loop method, CO 4 (6, 4, 4, 6, 4, 4, 6) sts. 120 (124, 136, 132, 136, 148, 144, 148) sts total: 26 (28, 32, 32, 34, 38, 38, 40) sts for front and back, 10 sts for each cable, 14 (14, 16, 14, 14, 16, 14, 14) sts for each sleeve.

Join for working in the rnd, pm to indicate the beg of rnd.

Rnd 1—raglan inc rnd: {Knit to marker, M1R, sm, work Bayside Cable patt over next 10 sts, sm, M1L} 4 times total. Knit to end. 8 sts inc.

Finished Measurements
Chest circumference: 32 (36, 40, 44, 48, 52, 56, 60)" / 81.5 (91.5, 101.5, 112, 122, 132, 142.5, 152.5) cm
Length: 24 (24¾, 25½, 26¼, 27, 27¾, 28½, 29¼)" / 61 (63, 65, 67, 68.5, 70.5, 72.5, 74.5) cm
Shown in size 32" / 81.5cm;
to be worn with 2–4"/ 5–10cm
of positive ease.

Materials
6 (7, 8, 9, 10, 11, 12, 13) skeins Quince & Company *Sparrow* (100% Organic Linen; 168 yds / 154m; 1¾ oz / 50g), undyed OR approx 950 (1100, 1275, 1425, 1600, 1800, 1975, 2175) yds / 875 (1025, 1175, 1325, 1475, 1650, 1825, 2000) m of fingering weight yarn, such as Louet *Euroflax Sport*.

US4 / 3.5mm 32" / 80cm circular needle, 16" / 40mm circular needle and set of 4 dpns

Stitch markers, cable needle, stitch holders, tapestry needle

Gauge
24 sts and 36 rows = 4" / 10cm in St st on US4 / 3.5mm needles or size needed to obtain gauge.

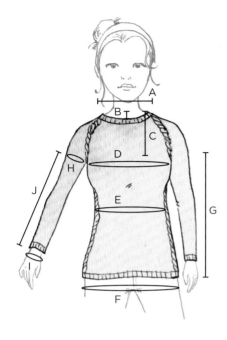

A	Back neck width	6¼ (6¾, 7, 7, 7¼, 7¾, 7¾, 8)"	
		16 (17, 18, 18, 18.5, 19.5, 19.5, 20.5) cm	
B	Front neck depth	1 (1, 1¼, 1¼, 1¼, 1½, 1½, 1½)"	
		2.5 (2.5, 3, 3, 3, 3.5, 3.5, 3.5) cm	
C	Yoke depth	6¼ (7, 7¾, 8½, 9¼, 10, 10¾, 11½)"	
		16 (18, 19.5, 21.5, 23.5, 25.5, 27.5, 29) cm	
D	Chest circ	32 (36, 40, 44, 48, 52, 56, 60)"	
		81.5 (91.5, 101.5, 112, 122, 132, 142, 152.5) cm	
E	Waist circ	30¾ (34¾, 38¾, 42¾, 46¾, 50¾, 54¾, 58¾)"	
		78 (88, 98, 108.5, 118.5, 128.5, 139, 149) cm	
F	Hip circ	33¼ (37¼, 41¼, 45¼, 49¼, 53¼, 57¼, 61¼)"	
		84.5 (95, 105, 115, 125.5, 135.5, 145.5, 156) cm	
G	Side length	18" / 45.5cm	
H	Upper sleeve circ	10¾ (12¼, 14, 15¾, 17¼, 19, 20¾, 22¼)"	
		27 (31.5, 35.5, 40, 44, 48.5, 52.5, 56.5) cm	
I	Cuff circ	6¾ (7¼, 8, 8¾, 9¼, 10, 10¾, 11¼)"	
		17 (18.5, 20.5, 22, 23.5, 25.5, 27, 29) cm	
J	Sleeve length	18" / 45.5cm	

Rnd 2: {Knit to marker, sm, work Bayside Cable patt over next 10 sts, sm} 4 times. Knit to end.

Rep last two rnds 21 (24, 27, 31, 35, 37, 42, 45) times more, switching to longer circular needle when desired. 296 (324, 360, 388, 424, 452, 488, 516) sts total: 70 (78, 88, 96, 106, 114, 124, 132) sts for front and back, 10 sts for each cable, 58 (64, 72, 78, 86, 92, 100, 106) sleeve sts.

Work as est until yoke measures 6¼ (7, 7¾, 8½, 9¼, 10, 10¾, 11½)" / 16 (18, 19.5, 21.5, 23.5, 25.5, 27.5, 29) cm from CO edge.

Body
DIVIDE SLEEVES FROM BODY
Next row (RS): {Knit to marker, sm, work Bayside Cable patt over next 10 sts, sm, place 58 [64, 72, 78, 86, 92, 100, 106] sleeve sts on a holder, CO 6 [10, 12, 16, 18, 22, 24, 28] underarm sts, sm, work cable chart over next 10 sts, sm} 2 times total. Knit to end. 192 (216, 240, 264, 288, 312, 336, 360) sts.

Cont in the rnd, work as est over body sts for 3" / 7.5cm.

Dec rnd: {Knit to marker, sm, work Bayside Cable patt over next 10 sts, sm, k2tog, knit to 2 sts before marker, ssk, sm, work Bayside Cable patt over next 10 sts, sm} 2 times total. Knit to end. 4 sts dec.

Rep dec rnd every 3" / 7.5cm once more. 184 (208, 232, 256, 280, 304, 328, 352) sts.

Work as est for 1" / 2.5cm.

Inc rnd: {Knit to marker, sm, work cable chart over next 10 sts, sm, M1R, knit to marker, M1L, sm, work cable chart over next 10 sts, sm} 2 times total. Knit to end. 4 sts inc.

Rep inc rnd every 3" / 7.5cm 3 times more. 200 (224, 248, 272, 296, 320, 344, 368) sts.

Ribbing setup rnd: {K2, p2} rep.

Cont in k2, p2 rib for 10 rnds. BO loosely in rib.

Sleeves
Divide held sleeve sts evenly over 3 dpns. With RS facing, k58 (64, 72, 78, 86, 92, 100, 106) sleeve sts, then pick up and knit 6 (10, 12, 16, 18, 22, 24, 28) sts along CO sts at underarm, placing a marker in the middle of the picked up sts to mark the beg of the rnd. Join for working in the rnd. 64 (74, 84, 94, 104, 114, 124, 134) sts.

Work even in St st for 11 rnds.

Dec rnd: K1, ssk, knit to last 3 sts, k2tog, k1. 2 sts dec.

Rep dec rnd every 12 (10, 8, 8, 6, 6, 6, 6) rnds 11 (10, 15, 6, 20, 14, 8, 2) times, then every 0 (8, 6, 6, 4, 4, 4, 4) rnds 0 (4, 2, 14, 3, 12, 21, 30) times more. 40 (44, 48, 52, 56, 60, 64, 68) sts.

Work even until sleeve measures 17" / 43cm from underarm edge or desired length.

Ribbing setup rnd: {K2, p2} rep.

Cont in k2, p2 rib for 10 rnds. BO loosely in rib.

Finishing
COLLAR
With shorter circular needle, pick up and knit 96 (104, 108, 104, 112, 116, 112, 120) sts around neck edge. Join to work in the rnd, pm.

Ribbing setup rnd: {K2, p2} rep.

Cont in k2, p2 rib for 10 rnds. BO loosely in rib.

Weave in all ends to the WS. Wet block to measurements.

Bayside Cable Chart

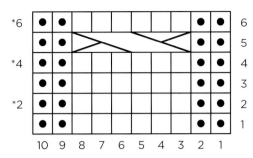

* applies only to WS rows when worked flat

knit on RS, purl on WS

purl on RS, knit on WS

C6F: Cable 6 Front. Sl 3 sts to cn and hold to front, k3, then k3 from cn.

Worked flat

Rows 1 and 3: P2, k6, p2.

Rows 2 and 4: K2, p6, k2.

Row 5: P2, C6F, p2.

Row 6: K2, p6, k2.

Worked in the round

Rnds 1–4: P2, k6, p2.

Rnd 5: P2, C6F p2.

Rnd 6: P2, k6, p2.

Living on the Central Coast for most of my life, I have grown accustomed to seeing oak trees... everywhere. But none of them quite compare to the mystical, twisted oaks in the Los Osos Oaks State Reserve.

Once home to the Chumash Indians, the meandering trails of the forest lead you through the ancient oaks estimated to be between 600 and 800 years old. The trunks of the trees have contorted and twisted throughout their long lives, creating the most unusual and eerie shapes. Additionally, many of the oaks are draped with long and lacy moss that sways in the cool ocean breeze; this only adds to their character.

Oaks State Reserve

LOS OSOS, CALIFORNIA

MOONSTONE BEACH BOARDWALK

1

101

ATASCADERO

SHELL CREEK ROAD

MORRO STRAND BEACH

SAN LUIS OBISPO

OAKS STATE RESERVE

MONTAÑA DE ORO

1

One would think that trees such as these would only exist in story-books. As a child, I remember walking through the reserve for the first time with my Dad and feeling as though I had been transported to an enchanted fairy tale land. Each tree was so old, with so much history and personality; it felt as though they could come alive at any moment. I wonder what secrets they could tell us of what life was like on the California coast 800 years ago.

Long draping moss
swaying in
the wind.

I hope to capture the essence of these enchanted trees in my Gnarled Oak Cardigan. I have always found the Reserve to be a very special part of the Central Coast, and I am so glad that the ancient oaks are being preserved for future generations to walk through and be inspired by.

27

Buttons made from oak branches.
Perfect for this project!

gnarled oak cardigan

A basic cardigan that features a stunning, embossed cabled oak leaf motif. *Gnarled Oak* is knit in one piece from the bottom up. The sleeves are knit separately and joined at the yoke.

Body

With larger circular needle, CO 192 (216, 236, 260, 280)[304, 324, 348, 368] sts.

Ribbing setup row (WS): P3, {k2, p2} rep across row until 5 sts remain, k2, p3.

Next row (RS): Work across 47 (53, 59, 65, 69)[75, 81, 87, 91] right front sts, pm, work 98 (110, 118, 130, 142)[154, 162, 174, 186] back sts, pm, work across remaining 47 (53, 59, 65, 69)[75, 81, 87, 91] left front sts.

Cont in est rib patt for 9 rows more. End on a WS row.

Next row (RS): Knit to first marker, sm, knit across back section dec 0 (1, 0, 1, 0)[1, 0, 1, 0] st or inc 1 (0, 1, 0, 1)[0, 1, 0, 1] st, sm, knit to end. 193 (215, 237, 259, 281)[303, 325, 347, 369] sts.

Work even in St st until work measures approx 5" / 12.5cm from CO edge. End on a WS row.

Dec row (RS): {Knit to 4 sts before marker, k2tog, k2, sm, k2, ssk} 2 times, knit to end. 4 sts dec.

Cont in St st for approx 5" / 12.5cm more. End on a WS row. Rep dec row. 185 (207, 229, 251, 273)[295, 317, 339, 361] sts.

Work even until piece measures 14½ (15, 15½, 16, 16½)[17, 17½, 18, 18½]" / 37 (38, 39.5, 40.5, 42)[43, 44.5, 45.5, 47] cm from CO edge. Do not cut yarn. Leave all sts unworked on circular needle and set aside.

Sleeves (Make 2)

With dpns, CO 44 (44, 48, 48, 52)[52, 56, 56, 60] sts. Divide sts evenly among dpns, and join into the rnd being careful not to twist your sts. Pm to mark the beg of the rnd.

Finished Measurements

Chest circumference (closed): 32 (35¾, 39½, 43, 46¾)[50½, 54, 57¾, 61½]" / 81.5 (91, 100, 109.5, 118.5)[128, 137.5, 146.5, 156] cm
Body length: 21½ (22½, 23½, 24½, 25½)[26½, 27½, 28½, 29½]" / 54.5 (57, 59.5, 62, 65)[67.5, 70, 72.5, 75] cm
Shown in size 35¾" / 91cm; to be worn with 0–2" / 0–5cm of positive ease.

Materials

5 (6, 6, 7, 8)[8, 9, 10, 11] skeins Pigeon-roof Studios *Cassiopeia DK* (75% Merino Wool, 15% Cashmere, 10% Silk; 260 yds / 238m; 4½ oz / 125g) in Juniper OR 1150 (1300, 1425, 1600, 1800)[1950, 2150, 2350, 2550] yds / 1050 (1200, 1300, 1475, 1650)[1775, 1975, 2150, 2325] m of DK weight wool blend, such as Madelinetosh *Tosh DK* or Madelinetosh *Tosh Merino DK*.

US5 / 3.75mm 32" / 80cm circular needle, set of 5 dpns, optional 2nd circular needle
US4 / 3.5mm 32" / 80cm circular needle

Stitch markers, 4 scraps of yarn to hold underarm sts, 1 safety pin marker, 2 stitch holders, cable needle, tapestry needle, 6 buttons 1"/ 2.5cm diameter, sewing needle and matching thread

Gauge

24 sts and 30 rows = 4" / 10cm in St st on US5 / 3.75mm needles or size needed to obtain gauge.

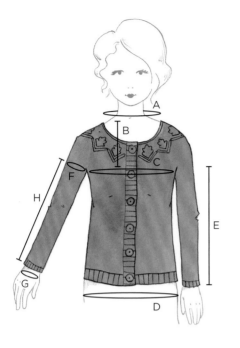

Neck, chest and hip circumferences are measured closed, with buttonband.

A	Neck circ	16¼ (17¾, 17¾, 19¼, 19¼)[20¾, 20¾, 22¼, 22¼]"
		41.5 (45, 45, 49, 49)[52.5, 52.5, 56.5, 56.5] cm
B	Yoke depth	6¾ (7¼, 7¾, 8¼, 8¾)[9¼, 9¾, 10¼, 10¾]"
		17 (18.5, 19.5, 21, 22)[23.5, 25, 26, 27.5] cm
C	Chest circ	32 (35¾, 39½, 43, 46¾)[50½, 54, 57¾, 61½]"
		81.5 (91, 100, 109.5, 118.5)[128, 137.5, 146.5, 156] cm
D	Hip circ	33½ (37, 40¾, 44½, 48)[51¾, 55½, 59, 62¾]"
		85 (94, 103.5, 113, 122)[131.5, 141, 150, 159.5] cm
E	Side length	14½ (15, 15½, 16, 16½)[17, 17½, 18, 18½]"
		37 (38, 39.5, 40.5, 42)[43, 44.5, 45.5, 47] cm
F	Upper sleeve circ	11¾ (12¾, 13¾, 14¾, 15¾)[16¾, 17¾, 18¾, 19¾]"
		29.5 (32, 34.5, 37.5, 40)[42.5, 45, 47.5, 50] cm
G	Cuff circ	7¼ (7¼, 8, 8, 8¾)[8¾, 9¼, 9¼, 10]"
		18.5 (18.5, 20.5, 20.5, 22)[22, 23.5, 23.5, 25.5] cm
H	Sleeve length	17½" / 44.5cm

Ribbing setup rnd: {K2, p2} rep.

Work in est rib patt for 10 rnds more. Knit 2 rnds.

Inc rnd: K1, M1R, knit to 1 st rem, M1L, k1. 2 sts inc.

Rep Inc rnd every 6 (6, 6, 4, 4)[4, 4, 4, 4] rnds 3 (15, 10, 3, 6)[15, 18, 27, 28] times more, then every 8 (0, 8, 6, 6)[6, 6, 0, 0] rnds 9 (0, 6, 16, 14)[8, 6, 0, 0] times more. 70 (76, 82, 88, 94)[100, 106, 112, 118] sts.

Work even in St st until sleeve measures 17½" / 44.5cm from CO edge.

Divide sts as follows: Slide first and last 7 (8, 9, 10, 11)[12, 13, 14, 15] sts of the rnd onto a scrap piece of yarn. Slide the remaining 56 (60, 64, 68, 72)[76, 80, 84, 88] sleeve sts onto a stitch holder. Cut yarn, leaving a long tail.

Yoke
JOIN SLEEVES TO BODY
With larger circular needle, k38 (43, 48, 53, 56)[61, 66, 71, 74] right front sts, slip next 14 (16, 18, 20, 22)[24, 26, 28, 30] underarm sts (half from right front and half from back) onto scrap piece of yarn, removing marker as you go. Hold sleeve to body with underarm sts together and with RS facing, k56 (60, 64, 68, 72)[76, 80, 84, 88] sleeve sts, then k81 (89, 97, 105, 117)[125, 133, 141, 153] sts for back. Slip next 14 (16, 18, 20, 22)[24, 26, 28, 30] underarm sts (half from back and half from left front) onto another scrap piece of yarn, removing marker as you go. Holding second sleeve in place as before, k56 (60, 64, 68, 72)[76, 80, 84, 88] sleeve sts, then k38 (43, 48, 53, 56)[61, 66, 71, 74] left front sts. Mark this joining row with a safety pin marker. 269 (295, 321, 347, 373)[399, 425, 451, 477] yoke sts.

The sleeves are now attached to the sweater body, while the live underarm sts are being held by scrap yarn to be grafted together later.

NOTE: It may be helpful to knit with the extra larger needle until several rows from the joining row have been worked. Your work will be very tight at first and using the extra needle to knit with makes it easier to maneuver.

SIZES 39½ (43, 46¾, 50½, 54, 5 7¾, 61½)" / 100 (109.5, 118.5, 128, 137.5, 146.5, 156) CM ONLY
Work even until yoke measures 1" / 2.5cm from joining row. End on a WS row. K9 (10, 10, 11, 11, 12, 12), k2tog, {k10 (11, 12, 13, 14, 15, 16), k2tog} until 10 (10, 11, 11, 12, 12, 13) sts remain, knit to end. 295 (321, 347, 373, 399, 425, 451) sts.

SIZES 46¾ (50½, 54, 5 7¾, 61½)" / 118.5 (128, 137.5, 146.5, 156) CM ONLY
Work even until yoke measures 2" / 5cm from joining row. End on a WS row. K10 (11, 12, 12), k2tog, {k11 (12, 13, 14, 15), k2tog} until 10 (10, 11, 11, 12) sts remain, knit to end. 321 (347, 373, 399, 425) sts.

SIZES 54 (57¾, 61½)" / 1 37.5 (146.5, 156) CM ONLY
Work even until yoke measures 3" / 7.5cm from joining row. End on a WS row. K10 (11, 11), k2tog, {k12 (13, 14), k2tog} until 11 (11, 12) sts remain, knit to end. 347 (373, 399) sts.

SIZE 61½" / 156 CM ONLY
Work even until yoke measures 4" / 10cm from joining row. End on a WS row. K11, k2tog, {k13, k2tog} until 11 sts remain, knit to end. 373 sts.

ALL SIZES
Work even until yoke measures ¾ (1¼, 1¾, 2¼, 2¾)[3¼, 3¾, 4¼, 4¾]" / 2 (3, 4.5, 5.5, 7)[8.5, 9.5, 11, 12] cm from joining row. End on a WS row.

WORK SHORT ROW SHAPING
Short row 1 (RS): Knit until 38 (43, 43, 48, 48)[53, 53, 56, 56] sts remain, w&t.
Short row 2 (WS): Purl until 38 (43, 43, 48, 48)[53, 53, 56, 56] sts remain, w&t.
Short row 3 (RS): Knit to previously wrapped st, pick up and knit wrap, k3 (4, 4, 5, 5)[6, 6, 6, 6], w&t.
Short row 4 (WS): Purl to previously wrapped st, pick up and purl wrap, p3 (4, 4, 5, 5)[6, 6, 6, 6], w&t.

Rep short rows 3 and 4 twice more.

Next row (RS): Knit, picking up and knitting remaining unworked wrapped st.
Next row (WS): Purl, picking up and purling remaining unworked wrapped st.

Work rows 1–29 of Gnarled Oak patt following the chart or written instructions.

Next row: Knit, dec 4 sts evenly across row. 90 (99, 99, 108, 108)[117, 117, 126, 126] sts.

Switch to smaller circular needle. Knit 5 rows.

BO all sts.

Finishing
BUTTONBAND
With smaller circular needle and RS facing, start at the neck edge and pick up and knit 128 (128, 128, 132, 132)[132, 136, 136, 136] sts along left front edge.

Ribbing setup row (WS): P3, {k2, p2} until 5 sts remain, k2, p3.

Work in est rib patt for 10 rows more.

BO in rib.

BUTTONHOLE BAND
With smaller circular needle and RS facing, start at the bottom CO edge and pick up and knit 128 (128, 128, 132, 132)[132, 136, 136, 136] sts along right front edge.

Ribbing setup row (WS): P3, {k2, p2} until 5 sts remain, k2, p3.

Work in est rib patt for 4 rows more. End on a WS row.

Buttonhole row (RS): Work 7 (7, 7, 6, 6)[6, 6, 6, 6] sts in patt, BO 3 sts in patt, {work 18 (18, 18, 19, 19)[19, 20, 20, 20] sts in patt, BO 3 sts in patt} 5 times total. Work remaining 7 (7, 7, 7, 7)[7, 6, 6, 6] sts in patt.

Next row (WS): Work 7 (7, 7, 6, 6)[6, 6, 6, 6] sts in patt. Using backwards loop method, CO 3 sts. {Work 19 (19, 19, 20, 20)[20, 21, 21, 21] sts in patt, CO 3 sts} 5 times total. Work remaining 7 (7, 7, 7, 7)[7, 6, 6, 6] sts in patt.

Work in est rib patt for 4 rows more. BO in rib.

Slide held underarm sts onto 2 dpns and graft sts together using Kitchener stitch. Use yarn tails to stitch up any remaining holes. Sew buttons onto Button Band opposite buttonholes.

Weave in all ends on the WS. Wet block to measurements.

Gnarled Oak Chart

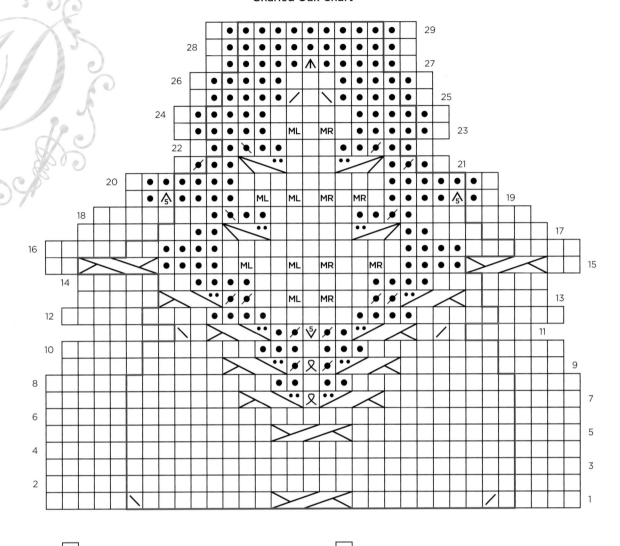

□	knit on RS, purl on WS
Ⴘ	k1 tbl
●	purl on RS, knit on WS
╱	k2tog
╲	ssk
⊿	p2tog on RS, k2tog on WS
⊾	k2tog tbl on WS
⋀	s2kp2
⃤₅	dec 5-to-1: Decrease 5 stitches to 1 stitch. Sl 3 sts together as if to knit, k2tog, then pass the 3 sl sts over.
⁵V	inc 1-to-5: Increase to 5 stitches from 1 stitch. (K1, yo) twice, then k1 into 1 st.

ML	M1L
MR	M1R
T4B	T4B: Twist 4 Back. Sl 2 sts to cn and hold to back, k2, then p2 from cn.
T4F	T4F: Twist 4 Front. Sl 2 sts to cn and hold to front, p2, then k2 from cn.
C5B	C5B: Cable 5 Back. Sl 3 sts to cn and hold to back, k2, then k3 from cn.
C5F	C5F: Cable 5 Front. Sl 2 sts to cn and hold to front, k3, then k2 from cn.
	Right Leaf Point: Sl 2 sts to cn and hold to back. Work next 3 sts on needle as follows: K3, turn, p3, turn, s2kp2. Then p2 from cn.
	Left Leaf Point: Sl 3 sts to cn and hold to front, then p2. Work next 3 sts on cn as follows: K3, turn, p3, turn, s2kp2.
□	patt rep

The blending of green and brown tones in this yarn remind me of the colors of the forest.

Row 18 (WS): P5, {p2, k1, k2tog tbl, k2, p5, k2, k2tog, k1, p3} 10 (11, 11, 12, 12)[13, 13, 14, 14] times, p4. 189 (207, 207, 225, 225)[243, 243, 261, 261] sts.

Row 19: K1, p1, {work dec 5-to-1, p4, k1, M1R, k1, M1R, k1, M1L, k1, M1L, k1, p4} 10 (11, 11, 12, 12)[13, 13, 14, 14] times, work dec 5-to-1, p1, k1. 185 (203, 203, 221, 221) [239, 239, 257, 257] sts.

Row 20 (WS): P1, k2, {k4, p9, k5} 10 (11, 11, 12, 12)[13, 13, 14, 14] times, k1, p1.

Row 21: K1, p1, {p2tog, p1, work Right Leaf Point, k3, work Left Leaf Point, p2} 10 (11, 11, 12, 12)[13, 13, 14, 14] times, p2tog, k1. 134 (147, 147, 160, 160)[173, 173, 186, 186] sts.

Row 22 (WS): P1, k1, {k1, k2tog tbl k2, p3, k2, k2tog, k1} 10 (11, 11, 12, 12)[13, 13, 14, 14] times, k1, p1. 114 (125, 125, 136, 136)[147, 147, 158, 158] sts.

Row 23: K1, p1, {p4, k1, M1R, k1, M1L, k1, p4} 10 (11, 11, 12, 12)[13, 13, 14, 14] times, p1, k1. 134 (147, 147, 160, 160)[173, 173, 186, 186] sts.

Rows 24 and 26: Work even

Row 25: K1, p1, {p4, ssk, k1, k2tog, p4} 10 (11, 11, 12, 12)[13, 13, 14, 14] times, p1, k1. 114 (125, 125, 136, 136)[147, 147, 158, 158] sts.

Row 27: K1, p1, {p4, s2kp2, p4} 10 (11, 11, 12, 12)[13, 13, 14, 14] times, p1, k1. 94 (103, 103, 112, 112)[121, 121, 130, 130] sts.

Row 28: P1, knit to last st, p1.

Row 29: K1, purl to last st, k1.

Row 1 (RS): K4, {k1, k2tog, k8, C5B, k8, ssk} 10 (11, 11, 12, 12)[13, 13, 14, 14] times, k5. 249 (273, 273, 297, 297)[321, 321, 345, 345] sts.

Rows 2, 3, 4, 6, 8, 10, 12, 14 and 16: Work even.

Row 5: K4, {k10, C5B, k9} 10 (11, 11, 12, 12)[13, 13, 14, 14] times, k5.

Row 7: K4, {k8, T4B, k1 tbl, T4F, k7} 10 (11, 11, 12, 12)[13, 13, 14, 14] times, k5.

Row 9: K4, {k6, T4B, p2tog, k1 tbl, p2tog, T4F, k5} 10 (11, 11, 12, 12)[13, 13, 14, 14] times, k5. 229 (251, 251, 273, 273)[295, 295, 317, 317] sts.

Row 11: K4, {k1, k2tog, k1, T4B, p1, p2tog, work inc 1-to-5, p2tog, p1, T4F, k1, ssk}10 (11, 11, 12, 12)[13, 13, 14, 14] times, k5.

Row 13: K4, {k1, T4B, p2tog twice, k2, M1R, k1, M1L, k2, p2tog twice, T4F} 10 (11, 11, 12, 12)[13, 13, 14, 14] times, k5. 209 (229, 229, 249, 249)[269, 269, 289, 289] sts.

Row 15: K2, C5B, {p4, k1, M1R, k2, M1R, k1, M1L, k2, M1L, k1, p4, C5F} 10 (11, 11, 12, 12)[13, 13, 14, 14] times, k2. 249 (273, 273, 297, 297)[321, 321, 345, 345] sts.

Row 17: K4, {k3, p2, work Right Leaf Point, k5, work Left Leaf Point, p2, k2} 10 (11, 11, 12, 12)[13, 13, 14, 14] times, k5. 209 (229, 229, 249, 249)[269, 269, 289, 289] sts.

Two Lights State Park

CAPE ELIZABETH, MAINE

TWO LIGHTS STATE PARK

On a summer day in Maine you might not expect to need a sweater. In downtown Port-land, it can be a hot day that calls for shorts and flip flops.

But take a drive out to Two Lights State Park and you will be surprised by the change in temperature. I am... every time! It's no wonder, as you're standing at the very tip of a peninsula that sticks out into the ocean. The cool breezes that blow off the rocky coast inspired the **Rocky Coast Cardigan***. With its wide collar and cozy cables, this cardigan, knit in a warm yet light aran weight yarn, helps keep out the windy afternoon chill.*

Two Lights State Park is named for the two nearby lighthouses called the Cape Elizabeth Lights, *the first twin lighthouses built in Maine back in 1828. They overlook Casco Bay and the open Atlantic. The first time I visited the park was with a storm-chasing friend, as there can be especially large surf here on a stormy day. Walking out onto the shelves of rocks that lead toward the crashing waves was an exhilarating experience.*

34

Drive to the end of Two Lights Road and you'll find The Lobster Shack, *a small, family-run eatery with the best lobster rolls and fried seafood. Local and visiting families carry their meal, including sodas from inside or a bottle of wine from home, to one of the scores of picnic tables to enjoy the million dollar view. We often come here with family or friends. After an enjoyable meal and maybe a few group photos, everyone disperses over the rocks. I like to take this opportunity to fold my arms and look out at the vastness of the ocean, filled with appreciation for all the good things in life.*

The park has shelves of rocks which you can explore for hours!

I wanted the perfect worsted weight
   in a classic shade of white — this is it!
so warm, yet so light and airy.

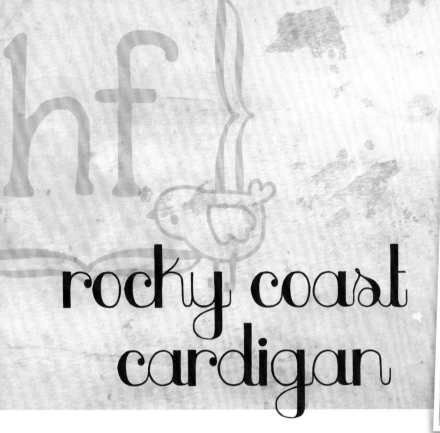

rocky coast cardigan

This cardigan offers real cabled comfort on a brisk New England day. Worked from the top down in a classic cable pattern that's easy to memorize. The collar is picked up and worked last.

Yoke
With larger circular needle, CO 58 (60, 62, 64, 66, 68, 70, 72) sts.

Setup row (WS): P3 left front sts, pm, p6 sleeve sts, pm, p40 (42, 44, 46, 48, 50, 52, 54) back sts, pm, p6 sleeve sts, pm, p3 right front sts.

ESTABLISH RAGLAN INCREASES
Raglan Inc row (RS): {Knit to 1 st before marker, M1R, k1, sm, k1, M1L} 4 times total, knit to end. 8 sts inc.

Purl 1 WS row.

ESTABLISH CABLE STITCH PATTERN ON BACK AND SLEEVES
Row 1 (RS): Knit to 1 st before marker, M1R, k1, sm, k1, M1L, work Cable Stitch patt over 6 sts, M1R, k1, sm, k1, M1L, k2 (3, 4, 2, 3, 4, 2, 3) sts, work Cable Stitch patt over 36 (36, 36, 42, 42, 42, 48, 48) sts, k2 (3, 4, 2, 3, 4, 2, 3) sts, M1R, k1, sm, k1, M1L, work Cable Stitch patt over 6 sts, M1R, k1, sm, k1, M1L, knit to end.
Rows 2–8: Work in patt as est, working raglan inc row every RS row and working additional reps of Cable Stitch patt as sts become available.

ESTABLISH CABLE STITCH PATTERN ON FRONTS
Row 9 (RS): K1, work Cable Stitch over 6 sts, M1R, k1, sm, work raglan inc row and Cable Stitch patt as est to last marker, sm, k1, M1L, work cable patt over 6 sts, k1.

Cont working cable patt as est, rep raglan inc row every RS row 8 (10, 12, 14, 16, 18, 20, 22) more times.

Finished Measurements
Chest circumference: 36 (40, 43, 48, 52, 55, 60, 64)″ / 91.5 (101.5, 109, 122, 132, 139.5, 152.5, 162.5) cm
Length: 23 (24, 25, 26, 27, 28, 29, 30)″ / 58.5 (61, 63, 66, 68.5, 71, 74, 76) cm
Shown in size 40″ / 112cm;
to be worn with 4–6″ / 10–15cm
of positive ease.

Materials
8 (9, 11, 12, 14, 15, 17, 18] skeins
The Fibre Company *Organik* (70% Organic Merino, 15% Baby Alpaca, 15% Silk; 98 yds / 90m; 1¾ oz / 50g) in Arctic Tundra OR 800 (900, 1100, 1200, 1400, 1500, 1700, 1800 yds / 725 (825, 1000, 1100, 1275, 1375, 1550, 1650) m of worsted weight yarn, such as Malabrigo *Worsted.*

US10½ / 6.5mm 32″ / 80cm circular needle and set of 4 dpns
US9 / 5.5mm 32″ / 80cm circular needle and set of 4 dpns

Stitch markers, cable needle, stitch holders, tapestry needle

Gauge
16 sts and 20 rows = 4″ / 10cm in Cable Stitch patt on US10½ / 6.5mm needles or size needed to obtain gauge.

WORK RAGLAN INCREASES ON SLEEVES ONLY

Raglan Sleeve Inc Row (RS): K1, {work in patt as est to m, sm, k1, M1L, working additional reps of Cable Stitch patt as sts become available, work in patt as est to 1 st before m, M1R, k1, sm} twice, work in patt as est to last st, k1.

Cont working cable patt as est, rep raglan sleeve inc row every RS row 3 more times.

End on row 2 (6, 2, 6, 2, 6, 2, 6) of cable patt. 186 (204, 222, 240, 258, 276, 294, 312) sts: 17 (19, 21, 23, 25, 27, 29, 31) for each front, 42 (46, 50, 54, 58, 62, 66, 70) sleeve sts, 68 (74, 80, 86, 92, 98, 104, 110) back sts.

Body
DIVIDE SLEEVES FROM BODY

Next row (RS): {Work in patt to marker, place sleeve sts on a holder, CO 4 (5, 6, 10, 11, 12, 16, 17) sts} twice, work in patt to end. 110 (122, 134, 152, 164, 176, 194, 206) sts.

Work in patt until body measures 13 (13¼, 13¼, 13½, 13¾, 14, 14¼, 14¼)" / 33 (33.5, 33.5, 34.5, 35, 35.5, 36, 36) cm from underarm or 3½" / 9cm less than desired length, dec 0 (0, 0, 2, 2, 2, 0, 0) sts evenly

on last row. End on a WS row. 110 (122, 134, 150, 162, 174, 194, 206) sts.

Switch to smaller circular needle.

Ribbing setup row (RS): {K2, p2} rep to last 2 sts, k2.

Cont in est rib patt for 19 rows more.

BO loosely in rib.

Sleeves

Divide 42 (46, 50, 54, 58, 62, 66, 70) held sleeve sts evenly over 3 larger dpns. Work row 3 (7, 3, 7, 3, 7, 3, 7) of cable patt as est, then with a fourth dpn, pick up and knit 4 (6, 6, 10, 12, 12, 16, 18) sts along underarm edge, placing marker in middle of the picked up sts to mark the beg of the rnd. Join for working in the rnd. 46 (52, 56, 64, 70, 74, 82, 88) sts.

Work 11 (7, 7, 7, 5, 5, 3, 3) rnds in patt, working as many sts in cable patt as possible and the remaining sts in St st.

Dec rnd: K1, ssk, work in patt to last 3 sts, k2tog, k1. 2 sts dec.

Rep dec rnd every 12 (8, 8, 8, 6, 6, 4, 4) rnds 4 (7, 7, 1, 5, 1, 14, 11) times more, then every 0 (0, 0, 6, 4, 4, 2, 2) rnds 0 (0, 0, 8,

7, 13, 2, 8) times more. 32 (32, 36, 36, 40, 40, 44, 44) sts. Work as est until sleeve measures 13" / 33cm from underarm or 3½" / 9cm less than desired length.

Switch to smaller dpns.

Work k2, p2 rib for 20 rnds.

BO loosely in rib.

Finishing
COLLAR

With smaller circular needle, RS facing and starting at the lower edge of the right front center, pick up 3 sts for every 4 rows along right front edge, pick up and knit 58 (60, 62, 64, 66, 68, 70, 72) sts along CO edge around neck, then cont down the left front, picking up 3 sts for every 4 rows. Specific st count does not matter as long as it is a multiple of 4 sts.

Ribbing setup row (WS): P3, {k2, p2} to last 2 sts, p1.

Cont in est rib patt for 19 rows more.

BO loosely in rib.

Weave in all ends on the WS. Wet block to measurements very gently, being mindful to not stretch out cables or rib.

Cable Stitch Chart

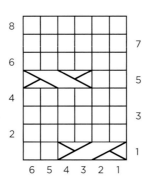

 knit on RS, purl on WS

C4B: Cable 4 Back. Sl 2 sts to cn and hold to back, k2, then k2 from cn.

C4F: Cable 4 Front. Sl 2 sts to cn and hold to front, k2, then k2 from cn.

Row 1: C4B, k2.

Row 2 and all even rows: Purl.

Rows 3 and 7: Knit.

Row 5: K2, C4F.

Row 8: Purl.

A Back neck width 10 (10½, 11, 11½, 12, 12½, 13, 13½)"
                   25.5 (26.5, 28, 29, 30.5, 32, 33, 34.5) cm

B Yoke depth   7¼ (8, 9, 9¾, 10½, 11¼, 12, 13)"
                   18.5 (20.5, 23, 25, 26.5, 28.5, 30.5, 33) cm

C Chest circ   36 (40, 43, 48, 52, 55, 60, 64)"
                   91.5 (101.5, 109, 122, 132, 139.5, 152.5, 162.5) cm

D Side length   13 (13¼, 13¼, 13½, 13¾, 14, 14¼, 14¼)"
                   33 (33.5, 33.5, 34.5, 35, 35.5, 36, 36) cm

E Ribbing length   3½" / 9cm

F Upper sleeve circ 11½ (13, 14, 16, 17½, 18½, 20½, 22)"
                   29 (33, 35.5, 40.5, 44.5, 47, 52, 56) cm

G Cuff circ   10 (10, 11, 11, 12, 12, 13, 13)"
                   25.5 (25.5, 28, 28, 30.5, 30.5, 33, 33) cm

H Sleeve length   16½" / 42cm

Shell Creek Road

SANTA MARGARITA, CALIFORNIA

Shell Creek Road is an unassuming country road off of the winding Highway 58. Named for the clam shell fossils found there, this area contains a small creek surrounded by grassy cow pastures with a backdrop of beautiful rolling California hills. For most of the year Shell Creek Road is comparable to any other road you might find in this area of the Central Coast. In the spring, however, it comes alive and reveals its hidden secrets.

The Shell Creek meadows put on one of the most spectacular wildflower displays in the entire Central Coast, making it an important yearly destination for flower enthusiasts, photographers, and picnicking families. The beautiful scenery and diversity of plants draw nature lovers from all over the country to this tiny road out in the middle of nowhere.

At the height of the season dozens of wildflower species literally carpet the ground you

A walking trail through the Coastal Tidy Tips at the height of the season.

walk on, although I most often see Coastal Tidy Tips, which is the yellow petaled flower that inspired my **Wildflower Cardigan**. The season can come and go quickly; there is only about a three week window to catch the wildflowers at their finest. This time of year is very exciting to the local community and it is common to see many families out enjoying the wildflowers, playing in the creek, and flying kites in the meadows. My family and friends attend a large picnic there during the spring. Every year I feel privileged to live so close to such an unexpectedly special place.

*I was immediately attracted
to this yarn and colorway
as soon as I saw it.
It really captures the essence
of springtime wildflowers
on the Central Coast.*

wildflower cardigan

A lightweight, ¾-sleeve cardigan perfect for layering on a brisk spring day. The sweater style itself is basic and flattering while the flower motif pockets and delicate edging add just enough feminine detail. *Wildflower* is knit in pieces from the bottom up and seamed together at the end.

Edging (Worked over a multiple of 10+2 sts)
Row 1 (WS): Purl.
Row 2 (RS): K2, {k1, slide st back to left hand needle, lift next 7 sts one at a time over this st and off the needle, yo twice, knit the first st again, k2} rep.
Row 3: P1, *p2tog, {k1, p1} twice in double yo, p1. Repeat from * to last st, p1.
Row 4: Knit.

Stitch count is now a multiple of 6+2 sts.

Pocket Linings (Make 2)
With US3 / 3.25mm needle, CO 19 sts.

Purl 1 WS row.

Inc row (RS): K1, kfb, knit to last st, kfb, k1. 2 sts inc.

Rep inc row every RS row 3 times more. 27 sts.

Work even until pocket measures 3½" / 9cm from CO edge. End on a WS row.

BO 2 sts, k22 sts, BO last 2 sts. Cut yarn. Place 23 remaining live sts onto stitch holder to be used later.

Back
With US1 / 2.25mm needle, CO 182 (202, 222, 242, 262)[282, 302, 322, 342] sts.

Work rows 1-4 of Edging. 110 (122, 134, 146, 158)[170, 182, 194, 206] sts.

Finished Measurements
Chest circumference (closed): 32¾ (36¼, 39½, 43, 46½) [49¾, 53¼, 56¾, 60¼]" / 83 (92, 100, 109, 118) [126.4, 135, 144, 153] cm
Body Length: 22¾ (23¾, 24¾, 25¾, 26¾) [27¾, 28¾, 29¾, 30¾]" / 58 (60.5, 63, 65.5, 68)[70.5, 73, 75.5, 78] cm
Shown in size 36¼" / 92cm; to be worn with 0-2"/ 0-5cm positive ease.

Materials
4 (5, 5, 6, 6)[7, 8, 8, 9] skeins Madelinetosh *Pashmina* (75% Merino Wool, 15% Silk, 10% Cashmere; 360 yds / 329m; 3½ oz / 100g) in Winter Wheat OR 1325 (1500, 1700, 1900, 2125)[2350, 2575, 2800, 3075] yds / 1200 (1375, 1575, 1750, 1950) [2150, 2375, 2575, 2800] m of sport weight wool blend, such as Blue Sky Alpacas *Sport Weight* or Debbie Bliss *Baby Cashmerino*.

US1 / 2.25mm 32" / 80cm circular needle
US2 / 2.75mm 32" / 80cm circular needle
US3 / 3.25mm 32" / 80cm circular needle

2 stitch holders, stitch markers, cable needle, 3 buttons ⅝" / 1.5mm diameter, tapestry needle, sewing needle and matching thread

Gauge
28 sts and 34 rows = 4" / 10cm in St st on US3 / 3.25mm needles or size needed to obtain gauge.

Switch to US3 / 3.25mm needle. Beg with a WS row, work in St st until piece measures 15½ (16, 16½, 17, 17½)[18, 18½, 19, 19½]" / 39 (41, 42, 43, 45)[46, 47, 48, 50] cm from CO edge. End on a WS row.

ARMHOLE SHAPING

BO 3 (4, 5, 6, 7)[8, 9, 10, 11] sts at the beg of next 2 rows, then 2 sts at the beg of next 0 (0, 0, 0, 6)[6, 12, 10, 14] rows. 104 (114, 124, 134, 132)[142, 140, 154, 156] sts.

Dec row (RS): K2, ssk, knit to 4 sts to the end, k2tog, k2. 2 sts dec.

Rep dec row every RS row 3 (5, 8, 11, 8)[12, 9, 15, 14] times more. 96 (102, 106, 110, 114)[116, 120, 122, 126] sts.

Work even in St st until armhole opening measures 6½ (7, 7½, 8, 8½)[9, 9½, 10, 10½]" / 17 (18, 19, 20, 22) [23, 24, 25, 27] cm. End on a WS row.

SHOULDER SHAPING

BO 7 (7, 8, 8, 9)[9, 9, 10, 10] sts at the beg of the next 4 (6, 2, 6, 2)[4, 6, 2, 4] rows, then 6 (0, 7, 0, 8)[8, 0, 9, 9] sts at the beg of the next 2 (0, 4, 0, 4)[2, 0, 4, 2] rows. 56 (60, 62, 62, 64)[64, 66, 66, 68] sts.

BO remaining back neck sts.

Right Front

With US1 / 2.25mm needle, CO 92 (102, 112, 122, 132)[142, 152, 162, 172] sts.

Work rows 1-4 of Edging. 56 (62, 68, 74, 80)[86, 92, 98, 104] sts.

Switch to US3 / 3.25mm needle. Beg with a WS row, work in St st until piece measures approx 2" / 5cm from CO edge. End on a RS row.

Setup row (WS): P22 (28, 34, 38, 44)[50, 54, 60, 66], pm, p27 {pocket sts}, pm, p7 (7, 7, 9, 9)[9, 11, 11, 11].

Work rows 1-32 of Wildflower Pocket over 27 pocket sts using the chart or written instructions. Work all sts on either side of markers in St st. Remove all markers on row 32.

JOIN POCKET LINING

Next row (RS): K9 (9, 9, 11, 11)[11, 13, 13, 13]. Adding a new strand of yarn, BO next 23 ribbed pocket sts, cut yarn. With original strand of yarn, knit across 23 pocket lining sts from stitch holder, knit to end.

Work even in St st until work measures 15½ (16, 16½, 17, 17½)[18, 18½, 19, 19½]" / 39.5 (40.5, 42, 43, 44.5)[45.5, 47, 48.5, 49.5] cm from CO edge. End on a RS row.

ARMHOLE AND NECK SHAPING

NOTE: Read entire section before starting. Some instructions are provided AT THE SAME TIME.

BO 3 (4, 5, 6, 7)[8, 9, 10, 11] sts on the next WS row, then 2 sts at the beg of next 0 (0, 0, 0, 3)[3, 6, 5, 7] WS rows. 53 (58, 63, 68, 67)[72, 71, 78, 79] sts.

Dec row (RS): Knit until 4 sts remain, k2tog, k2. 1 st dec.

Rep dec row every RS row 3 (5, 8, 11, 8)[12, 9, 15, 14] times more.

AT THE SAME TIME, when armhole measures ¾ (1¼, 1¾, 2¼, 2¾)[3¼, 3¾, 4¼, 4¾]" / 2 (3, 4.5, 5.5, 7)[8.5, 9.5, 11, 12] cm, shape neckline as follows:

BO 11 sts at the beg of next RS row, then 2 sts at the beg of next 5 RS rows. 28 (31, 33, 35, 37)[38, 40, 41, 43] sts.

Dec row (RS): K1, ssk, knit to end. 1 st dec.

Rep dec row every RS row 7 (9, 10, 10, 11)[11, 12, 12, 13] times more. 20 (21, 22, 24, 25)[26, 27, 28, 29] sts.

Work even in St st until armhole measures same as for back. End on a RS row.

SHOULDER SHAPING

BO 7 (7, 8, 8, 9)[9, 9, 10, 10] sts at the beg of the next 2 (3, 1, 3, 1)[2, 3, 1, 2] WS rows, then 6 (0, 7, 0, 8)[8, 0, 9, 9] sts at the beg of the next 1 (0, 2, 0, 2)[1, 0, 2, 1] WS row(s).

Left Front

With US1 / 2.25mm needle, CO 92 (102, 112, 122, 132)[142, 152, 162, 172] sts.

Work rows 1-4 of Edging. 56 (62, 68, 74, 80)[86, 92, 98, 104] sts.

Switch to US3 / 3.25mm needle. Beg with a WS row, work in St st until piece measures approx 2" / 5cm from CO edge. End on a RS row.

Set up row (WS): P7 (7, 7, 9, 9)[9, 11, 11, 11], pm, p27 {pocket sts}, pm, p22 (28, 34, 38, 44)[50, 54, 60, 66].

Work rows 1-32 Wildflower Pocket over next 27 pocket sts as for right front.

JOIN POCKET LINING

Next row (RS): K24 (30, 36, 40, 46)[52, 56, 62, 68]. Adding a new strand of yarn, BO next 23 ribbed pocket sts, cut yarn. With original strand of yarn, knit across 23 pocket lining sts from stitch holder, knit to end.

Work even in St st until work measures 15½ (16, 16½, 17, 17½)[18, 18½, 19, 19½]" / 39.5 (40.5, 42, 43, 44.5)[45.5, 47, 48.5, 49.5] cm from CO edge. End on a WS row.

ARMHOLE AND NECK SHAPING

NOTE: Read entire section before starting. Some instructions are provided AT THE SAME TIME.

BO 3 (4, 5, 6, 7)[8, 9, 10, 11] sts on the next RS row, then 2 sts at the beg of next 0 (0, 0, 0, 3)[3, 6, 5, 7] RS rows. 53 (58, 63, 68, 67)[72, 71, 78, 79] sts.

Dec row (RS): K2, ssk, knit to end. 1 st dec.

Rep dec row every RS row 3 (5, 8, 11, 8)[12, 9, 15, 14] times more.

AT THE SAME TIME, when armhole measures ¾ (1¼, 1¾, 2¼, 2¾)[3¼, 3¾, 4¼, 4¾]" / 2 (3, 4.5, 5.5, 7)[8.5, 9.5, 11, 12] cm, shape neckline as follows:

BO 11 sts at the beg of next WS row, then 2 sts at the beg of next 5 WS rows. 28 (31, 33, 35, 37)[38, 40, 41, 43] sts.

Wildflower Pocket Chart

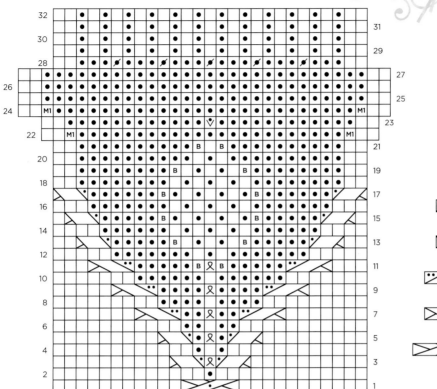

	knit on RS, purl on WS
⟨	k1 tbl on RS
•	purl on RS, knit on WS
⟋	p2tog on RS, k2tog on WS
⋁	pfb
M1	M1
B	MB: Make Bobble. (K1, p1, k1, p1, k1) in next st, turn, p5, turn, pass first 4 sts over the 5th st, knit 5th st tbl.
	T3B: Twist 3 Back. Sl 1 st to cn and hold to back, k2, then p1 from cn.
	T3F: Twist 3 Front. Sl 2 sts to cn and hold to front, p1, then k2 from cn.
	T4B: Twist 4 Back. Sl 2 sts to cn and hold to back, k2, then p2 from cn.
	T4F: Twist 4 Front. Sl 2 sts to cn and hold to front, p2, then k2 from cn.
	T5B: Twist 5 Back. Sl 3 sts to cn and hold to back, k2, then p1, k2 from cn.

Row 1 (RS): K11, T5B, k11.

Row 2 (WS): P13, k1, p13.

Row 3: K10, T3B, k1 tbl, T3F, k10.

Row 4: P12, k1, p1, k1, p12.

Row 5: K9, T3B, p1, k1 tbl, p1, T3F, k9.

Row 6: P11, k2, p1, k2, p11.

Row 7: K7, T4B, p2, k1 tbl, p2, T4F, k7.

Row 8: P9, k4, p1, k4, p9.

Row 9: K5, T4B, p4, k1 tbl, p4, T4F, k5.

Row 10: P7, k6, p1, k6, p7.

Row 11: K3, T4B, p5, MB, k1 tbl, MB, p5, T4F, k3.

Row 12: P5, k7, p1, k1, p1, k7, p5.

Row 13: K2, T3B, p5, MB, k1, {p1, k1} twice, MB, p5, T3F, k2.

Row 14: P4, k6, p1, {k1, p1} 3 times, k6, p4.

Row 15: K1, T3B, p5, MB, p1, {k1, p1} 3 times, MB, p5, T3F, k1.

Row 16: P3, k7, p1, {k1, p1} 3 times, k7, p3.

Row 17: T3B, p6, MB, p1, {k1, p1} 3 times, MB, p6, T3F.

Row 18: P2, k8, {p1, k1} 4 times, k7, p2.

Row 19: K2, p8, MB, k1, {p1, k1} 2 times, MB, p8, k2.

Row 20: P2, k10, p1, k1, p1, k10, p2.

Row 21: K2, p10, MB, k1, MB, p10, k2.

Row 22: P2, M1, k23, M1, p2. 29 sts.

Row 23: K2, p12, pfb, p12, k2. 30 sts.

Row 24: P2, M1, k26, M1, p2. 32 sts.

Row 25: K2, p28, k2.

Row 26: P2, k28, p2.

Row 27: K2, p28, k2.

Row 28: P2, {k3, k2tog} 5 times, k3, p2. 27 sts.

Row 29: K2, {p1, k1} 11 times, p1, k2.

Row 30: P2, {k1, p1} 11 times, k1, p2.

Row 31: K2, {p1, k1} 11 times, p1, k2.

Row 32: P2, {k1, p1} 11 times, k1, p2.

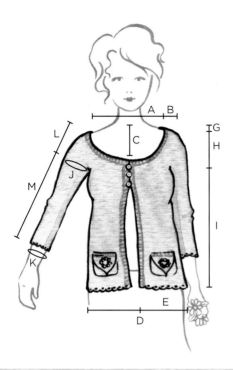

A Back neck width 8 (8½, 8¾, 8¾, 9¼)[9¼, 9½, 9½, 9¾]"
20.5 (22, 22.5, 22.5, 23)[23, 24, 24, 24.5] cm

B Shoulder width 2¾ (3, 3¼, 3½, 3½)[3¾, 3¾, 4, 4¼]"
7.5 (7.5, 8, 8.5, 9)[9.5, 10, 10, 10.5] cm

C Neck depth 6½" / 16.5cm

D Back width 15¾ (17½, 19¼, 20¾, 22½)[24¼, 26, 27¾, 29½]"
40 (44.5, 48.5, 53, 57.5)[61.5, 66, 70.5, 74.5] cm

E Front width 8 (8¾, 9¾, 10½, 11½)[12¼, 13¼, 14, 14¾]"
20.5 (22.5, 24.5, 27, 29)[31, 33.5, 35.5, 37.5] cm

G Shoulder height ¾" / 2cm

H Armhole height 6½ (7, 7½, 8, 8½)[9, 9½, 10, 10½]"
16.5 (18, 19, 20.5, 21.5)[23, 24, 25.5, 26.5] cm

I Side length 15½ (16, 16½, 17, 17½)[18, 18½, 19, 19½]"
39.5 (40.5, 42, 43, 44.5)[45.5, 47, 48.5, 49.5] cm

J Upper arm circ 9¾ (10½, 12¼, 13¼, 14¾)[15¾, 17½, 18, 19½]"
24.5 (27, 31, 33.5, 37.5)[40, 44.5, 45.5, 49.5] cm

K Sleeve cuff circ 8¾ (9¾, 10½, 10½, 11½)[11½, 12¼, 12¼, 13¼]"
22.5 (24.5, 27, 27, 29)[29, 31, 31, 33.5] cm

L Cap height 5½ (6, 6½, 7, 7½)[8, 8½, 9, 9½]"
13.5 (15.5, 16.5, 18, 19)[20.5, 21.5, 22.5, 24] cm

M Sleeve length 11" / 28cm

Dec row (RS): Knit until 3 sts remain, k2tog, k1. 1 st dec.

Rep dec row every RS row 7 (9, 10, 10, 11) [11, 12, 12, 13] times more. 20 (21, 22, 24, 25)[26, 27, 28, 29] sts.

Work even in St st until armhole measures same as for back. End on a WS row.

SHOULDER SHAPING

BO 7 (7, 8, 8, 9)[9, 9, 10, 10] sts at beg of the next 2 (3, 1, 3, 1)[2, 3, 1, 2] RS row(s), then 6 (0, 7, 0, 8)[8, 0, 9, 9] sts at beg of the next 1 (0, 2, 0, 2)[1, 0, 2, 1] RS row(s).

Sleeves (Make 2)

With US1 / 2.25mm needle, CO 102 (112, 122, 122, 132)[132, 142, 142, 152] sts.

Work rows 1–4 of Edging. 62 (68, 74, 74, 80)[80, 86, 86, 92] sts.

Switch to size US3 / 3.25mm needle. Beg with a WS row, work in St st for 17 (17, 7, 5, 5)[3, 3, 3, 3] rows. End on a WS row.

Inc row (RS): K1, M1R, knit to last st, M1L, k1. 2 sts inc.

Rep inc row every 34 (34, 16, 10, 8)[6, 6, 6, 4] rows 2 (2, 4, 8, 8)[13, 7, 3, 21] times more, then every 0 (0, 14, 0, 6)[4, 4, 4, 0] rows 0 (0, 1, 0, 3)[1, 10, 16, 0] time(s) more. 68 (74, 86, 92, 104)[110, 122, 126, 136] sts.

Work even in St st until piece measures 11" / 27.5cm from CO edge. End on a WS row.

SLEEVE CAP SHAPING

BO 3 (4, 5, 6, 7)[8, 9, 10, 11] sts at beg of the next 2 rows, then 2 sts at beg of the next 0 (0, 0, 0, 6)[6, 12, 10, 14] rows. 62 (66, 76, 80, 78)[82, 80, 86, 86] sts.

Dec row (RS): K2, ssk, knit to last 4 sts, k2tog, k2. 2 sts dec.

Rep dec row every RS row 8 (9, 25, 27, 26)[28, 27, 30, 30] times more, every 4th row 2 (3, 0, 0, 0)[0, 0, 0, 0] times more, then every RS row 8 (8, 0, 0, 0)[0, 0, 0, 0] times more. 24 sts.

Purl 1 WS row.

BO 2 sts at the beg of next 2 rows. BO 3 sts at the beg of next 2 rows. 14 sts.

BO remaining sts.

Finishing

Wet block pieces to measurements. Seam front and back shoulder sts together using yarn tails and tapestry needle.

NECKBAND

With US2 / 2.75mm needle and RS facing, start at the right side of the neck opening and pick up and knit 11 bound off sts from right front, 10 sts from right side bind off, 36 from right side neck sts, 57 (61, 63, 63, 65)[65, 67, 67, 69] sts from back neck, 36 left side neck sts, 10 sts from left side bind off, and 11 bound off sts from left front. 171 (175, 177, 177, 179) [179, 181, 181, 183] sts.

Next row (WS): P2, {k1, p1} rep until 1 st remains, p1.

Cont in est rib patt for 1" / 2.5cm.

BO in rib.

BUTTON BAND

With US2 / 2.75mm needle and RS facing, start at the neck edge and pick up sts at a rate of 3 sts per 4 rows along the left front edge. End on an odd number of sts.

Setup row (WS): {P1, k1} rep to last st, p1.

Cont in est rib patt for 6 rows more.

BO off in rib.

BUTTONHOLE BAND

With US2 / 2.75mm needle and RS facing, start at the bottom CO edge and pick up and knit the same number of sts along the right front as for the left front.

Row 1 (WS): {P1, k1} rep to last st, p1.
Rows 2 and 3: Work even in est rib patt.
Row 4 (RS): Work in patt until 28 sts remain. BO 2 sts in patt, {work 8 sts in patt, BO 2 sts in patt} 2 times, work last 3 sts in patt.
Row 5: Work in est rib patt across row.

Using backwards loop CO method, CO 2 sts over gaps.
Row 6 (RS): {K1, p1} rep to last st, k1.
Row 7: Work even in est rib patt.

BO in rib.

Set in sleeves and sew up sleeve and side seams using the mattress st. Sew pocket linings to sweater body on the WS using mattress st. Weave in all ends on the WS. Sew buttons onto Button Band opposite buttonholes.

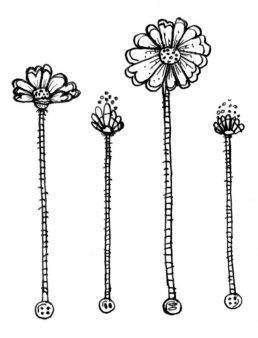

Willard Beach is part of Spring Point in South Portland, Maine. From its shore you see the Spring Point Ledge Lighthouse, which you can hike out to over a long rocky jetty. It's also at the edge of the Southern Maine Community College campus. My husband was attending this school when we first met, and I lived just a few blocks away. We've walked this beach many times in the 14 years since then.

Willard Beach

We are fortunate that in our area we have access to a lot of beaches, all of which have their unique charms. For me, Willard is the perfect beach for walking, whether for an early morning stroll or an evening ramble. The **Water's Edge Cardigan** *mimics the gentle curve of the Willard Beach shoreline, which is emphasized as the tide rolls in and out.*

In the past few years the community that surrounds the beach has grown in popularity. The Scratch Baking Company *has become the center of the neighborhood, and the sidewalks are bustling with friendly folk—mothers pushing strollers, grandparents on their daily constitutional, hipsters on bicycles. It pretty much goes without saying that if we're heading over to walk the beach, we're first stopping for a treat or coffee to carry with us. Willard is a full circle experience for me. It's where I started down the road to married life when I met my husband, and where I continue to spend time with my family today.*

48

Overlooking the foggy ocean on a late afternoon at Willard Beach.

The color of this hand-dyed yarn is Skerry, named after the rock formations
at the edge of fjords where seaweed grows.
Inspired by rocks, seaweed and cold northern waters, it's the right color for Water's Edge!

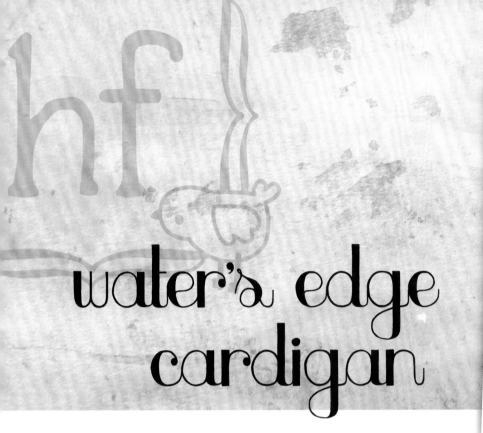

water's edge cardigan

A top-down cardigan with a well-placed pleat that flatters the waist. Short row shaping at the hem creates a slight curve, mimicking the shape of a shore line. With elbow-length sleeves, this a cardigan for all seasons!

Yoke

With circular needle, CO 60 (62, 64, 66, 68)[70, 72, 74, 76] sts.

Setup row (WS): P3 left front sts, pm, p10 sleeve sts, pm, p34 (36, 38, 40, 42)[44, 46, 48, 50] back sts, pm, p10 sleeve sts, pm, p3 right front sts.

Row 1 (RS): K1, M1L, {knit to 1 st before marker, M1R, k1, sm, k1, M1L} 4 times, knit to last st of row, M1R, k1. 10 sts inc.
Row 2 (WS): Purl.

Rep these two rows 20 (22, 24, 26, 28)[30, 32, 34, 36] times more. 270 (292, 314, 336, 358)[380, 402, 424, 446] sts.

DIVIDE SLEEVES FROM BODY
Row 1 (RS): K45 (49, 53, 57, 61)[65, 69, 73, 77], remove marker, place 52 (56, 60, 64, 68)[72, 76, 80, 84] sleeve sts on a holder, CO 1 (2, 3, 4, 5)[6, 7, 8, 9] sts, pm, CO 1 (2, 3, 4, 5)[6, 7, 8, 9] sts, k76 (82, 88, 94, 100)[106, 112, 118, 124], remove marker, place 52 (56, 60, 64, 68)[72, 76, 80, 84] sleeve sts on a holder, CO 1 (2, 3, 4, 5)[6, 7, 8, 9] sts, pm, CO 1 (2, 3, 4, 5)[6, 7, 8, 9] sts, knit to end. 170 (188, 206, 224, 242)[260, 278, 296, 314] sts.
Row 2 (WS): Purl.

Work even in St st for 8 (10, 12, 14, 16)[18, 20, 22, 24] rows.

Dec row (RS): {Knit to 3 sts before marker, k2tog, k1, sm, k1 ssk} 2 times, knit to end. 4 sts dec.

Rep dec row every 14 rows 2 times more. 158 (176, 194, 212, 230)[248, 266, 284, 302] sts.

Finished Size
Chest circumference: 34 (37½, 41¼, 44¾, 48½)[52, 55½, 59¼, 62¾]" / 86.5 (95.5, 104.5, 114, 123)[132, 141, 150.5, 159.5] cm
Length: 20¾ (21½, 22¾, 23½, 24¾) [25½, 26¾, 27½, 28¾]" / 52.5 (55, 57.5, 60, 63)[65, 68, 70, 73]
Shown in size 34" / 86.5cm; to be worn with 0–2" / 0–5cm positive ease.

Materials
5 (6, 7, 7, 8)[9, 10, 11, 12] skeins String Theory Hand Dyed Yarn *Caper Aran* (80% Merino, 10% Cashmere, 10% Nylon; 200 yds / 183m; 3½ oz / 100g) in Skerry OR 950 (1075, 1225, 1375, 1550)[1700, 1875, 2050, 2250] yds / 900 (1025, 1150, 1300, 1460) [1600, 1775, 1925, 2125] m of DK weight wool blend, such as Madelinetosh *Merino DK.*

US7 / 4mm 32" / 80cm circular needle and set of dpns

Stitch markers, stitch holders, tapestry needle

Gauge
20 sts and 28 rows = 4" / 10cm in St st on US7 / 4mm needles or size needed to obtain gauge.

Work even in St st for 8 rows.

CREATE PLEAT

Row 1 (RS): Using one of the dpns, pick up the st 6 rows below the next st on your left needle. Place it on your left needle and knit together with the next st. Rep across the row.
Row 2 (WS): Purl.
Row 3 (RS): {Kfb} to last st, k1. 315 (351, 387, 423, 459)[495, 531, 567, 603] sts.

Work even in St st until piece measures 5" / 12.5cm from pleat.

WORK SHORT ROWS

Short row 1 (RS): Knit to 2 sts from end of row, w&t.
Short row 2 (WS): Purl to 2 sts from end of row, w&t.
Short row 3: Knit to 2 sts from wrapped st, w&t.
Short row 4: Purl to 2 sts from wrapped st, w&t.

Rep last 2 rows 4 (4, 5, 5, 6)[6, 7, 7, 8] times more.

Next row (RS): Knit, picking up and knitting wraps.
Next row (WS): Purl, picking up and purling wraps.

Ribbing setup row (RS): {K1, p1} to last st, k1.

Work in est rib patt for 6 rows more.

BO in rib.

Sleeves

Divide 52 (56, 60, 64, 68)[72, 76, 80, 84] held sleeve sts evenly among dpns. Pick up and k2 (4, 6, 8, 10)[12, 14, 16, 18] sts from CO at underarm, placing marker in the middle of the 2 (4, 6, 8, 10)[12, 14, 16, 18] underarm sts, then knit to marker. 54 (60, 66, 72, 78)[84, 90, 96, 102] sts.

Work even in St st for 9 rnds.

Dec rnd (RS): K1, ssk, knit to last 3 sts, k2tog, k1. 2 sts dec.

Rep dec rnd every 10 rnds 3 times more. 46 (52, 58, 64, 70)[76, 82, 88, 94] sts.

Work even until sleeve measures 7" / 17.5cm, or 1" / 2.5cm shorter than desired length.

Ribbing setup rnd (RS): {K1, p1} rep around.

Work in est rib patt for 6 rnds more.

BO in rib.

Finishing

With circular needle, beginning at right front bottom edge, pick up and knit 2 sts for every 3 rows of the right front edge. Continue across the top of the right sleeve, across the back, then across the top of the left sleeve, picking up and knitting 1 st for every st. Finish by picking up and knitting 2 sts for every 3 rows along left front edge.

Work even in St st for 5 rows.

BO all sts.

Weave in ends on the WS. Wet block to measurements.

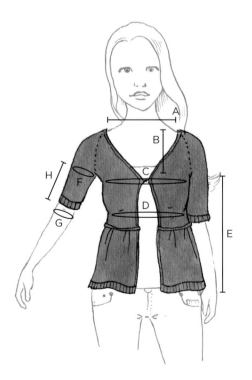

A	Back neck width	6¾ (7¼, 7.5, 8, 8½)[8¾, 9¼, 9½, 10]"
		17.5 (18.5, 19.5, 20.5, 21.5)[22.5, 23.5, 24.5, 25.5] cm
B	Yoke depth	6 (6½, 7¼, 7¾, 8¼)[8¾, 9½, 10, 10½]"
		15 (16.5, 18, 19.5, 21)[22.5, 24, 25.5, 27] cm
C	Chest circ	34 (37½, 41¼, 44¾, 48½)[52, 55½, 59¼, 62¾]"
		86.5 (95.5, 104.5, 114, 123)[132, 141, 150.5, 159.5] cm
D	Waist circ	31½ (35¼, 38¾, 42½, 46)[49½, 53¼, 56¾, 60½]"
		80.5 (89.5, 98.5, 107.5, 117)[126, 135, 144.5, 153.5] cm
E	Side length	13¾ (14, 14½, 14¾, 15½)[15¾, 16¼, 16½, 17¼]"
		35 (35.5, 37, 37.5, 39)[40, 41.5, 42, 43.5] cm
F	Upper sleeve circ	10¾ (12, 13¼, 14½, 15½)[16¾, 18, 19¼, 20½]"
		27.5 (30.5, 33.5, 36.5, 39.5)[42.5, 45.5, 49, 52] cm
G	Lower sleeve circ	9¼ (10½, 11.5, 12¾, 14)[15¼, 16½, 17½, 18¾]"
		23.5 (26.5, 29.5, 32.5, 35.5)[38.5, 41.5, 44.5, 48] cm
H	Sleeve length	8" / 20.5cm

ACCESSORIES

Montaña De Oro

LOS OSOS, CALIFORNIA

One of my favorite local destinations along California's coastline is the very diverse Montaña De Oro State Park. The winding road entering the park is flanked on either side by hundreds of enormous eucalyptus trees. Once planted for timber but never used, the trees remain undisturbed in nice, neat rows.

A short hike through the grove leads you towards the ocean. The shady, serene trail takes you over a creek and through beautiful wildflowers. Overhead you can hear the long slender leaves rustling as the wind carries the scent of eucalyptus through the air. This tranquil spot inspired my **Rustling Leaves Beret**, which features slanted leaves knit in a special yarn dyed with eucalyptus.

The view from the top of the cliffs.

As you walk along the trail, the leaf-lined path quickly turns to sand as you get closer to the Pacific Ocean. From the top of the cliffs you can travel down sandy paths to the beach, where Montaña De Oro is known for its magnificent tide pools. I have been visiting Montaña De Oro ever since I was a small child. I remember hiking through the eucalyptus-lined trails with my parents and climbing up the slippery rocks to peer into the tide pools. Those tide pools were an endless source of entertainment for me. How exciting it was to see starfish, sea anemone, and hermit crabs going about their daily lives in their natural environment! I will forever be amazed by how much there is to see and experience in this peaceful, local location. I plan on spending many more afternoons here with my son and daughter underneath the eucalyptus... and in the sand.

56

This beautiful green
colorway was actually
created from dried
eucalyptus leaves!

rustling leaves beret

Rustling Leaves is the perfect fall accessory. Knit from the bottom up, this beret features beautiful elongated leaves that slant in different directions as if they were rustling in the wind.

Cast On
With smaller circular needle, CO 144 sts. Pm and join in the rnd, being careful not to twist your sts.

Ribbing setup rnd: {K1, p1} rep.

Work in est rib for 1¼" / 3cm.

BERET BODY
Switch to larger circular needle. Work rnds 1-61 of Rustling Leaves patt, following the chart or written instructions.

Switch to dpns when work becomes too tight on the circular needle. End with 6 sts.

Next rnd: {K2tog, k1} rep. 4 sts

Finishing
Remove stitch marker. Slip all 4 sts onto 1 dpn and work 2 rnds of I-cord.

Cut yarn, thread tail onto tapestry needle and pass through remaining 4 live sts and cinch to close. Weave in all ends on the inside of the beret.

Wet block to measurements by stretching over a dinner plate.

Size
Stretches to fit a 19–22" / 43-56cm head circumference.

Finished Measurements
Brim circumference: approx 20" / 51cm after blocking
Diameter: approx 10" / 25cm across after blocking

Materials
1 skein Tactile Fiber Arts *Wild Crafted* (50% Superwash Merino Wool, 50% Tencel; 360 yds / 329m; 3½ oz / 100g) in Windfall Eucalyptus Leaves OR approx 175 yds / 160m of finger-ing weight wool or wool blend yarn, such as Malabrigo *Sock* or Madelinetosh *Tosh Sock*.

US3 / 3.25mm 16" / 40cm circular needle and set of dpns
US2 / 2.75mm 16" / 40cm circular needle

Stitch marker, tapestry needle

Gauge
28 sts and 34 rows = 4" / 10cm in St st on US3 / 3.25mm needles or size needed to obtain gauge.

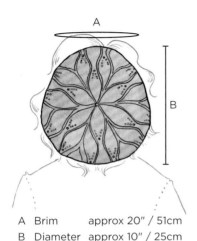

A Brim   approx 20" / 51cm
B Diameter approx 10" / 25cm

Rnd 1: {K1, p5} rep.

Rnd 2: {K1, p5} rep.

Rnd 3: {Work inc 1-to-3, p5, k1, p5} rep. 168 sts.

Rnd 4: Work even.

Rnd 5: {[K1, yo] twice, k1, p2tog, p3, k1, p3, p2tog} rep.

Rnd 6: Work even.

Rnd 7: {K2, yo, k1, yo, k2, p2tog, p2, k1, p2, p2tog} rep.

Rnd 8: Work even.

Rnd 9: {K3, yo, k1, yo, k3, p2tog, p1, k1, p1, p2tog} rep.

Rnd 10: Work even.

Rnd 11: {Ssk, k7, p2, k1, p2} rep. 156 sts.

Rnd 12: Work even.

Rnd 13: {Ssk, k6, p2, k1, p2} rep. 144 sts.

Rnd 14: Work even.

Rnd 15: {Ssk, k5, p2, work inc 1-to-3, p2} rep. 156 sts.

Rnd 16: Work even.

Rnd 17: {Ssk, k4, p2, [k1, yo] twice, k1, p2} rep. 168 sts.

Rnd 18: Work even.

Rnd 19: {Ssk, k3, p2, k2, yo, k1, yo, k2, p2} rep. 180 sts.

Rnd 20: Work even.

Rnd 21: {Ssk, k2, p2, k3, yo, k1, yo, k3, p2} rep. 192 sts.

Rnd 22: Work even.

Rnd 23: {Ssk, k1, p2, k7, k2tog, p2} rep. 168 sts.

Rnd 24: Work even.

Rnd 25: {Ssk, p2, k6, k2tog, p2} rep. 144 sts.

Rnd 26: Work even.

Rnd 27: {Work inc 1-to-3, p2, k5, k2tog, p2} rep. 156 sts.

Rnd 28: Work even.

Rnd 29: {[K1, yo] twice, k1, p2, k4, k2tog, p2} rep. 168 sts.

Rnd 30: Work even.

Rnd 31: {K2, yo, k1, yo, k2, p2, k3, k2tog, p2} rep. 180 sts.

Rnd 32: Work even.

Rnd 33: {K3, yo, k1, yo, k3, p2, k2, k2tog, p2} rep. 192 sts.

Rnd 34: Work even.

Rnd 35: {Ssk, k7, p2, k1, k2tog, p2, k7, k2tog, p2, k1, k2tog, p2} rep. 168 sts.

Rnd 36: Work even.

Rnd 37: {Ssk, k6, p2, k2tog, p2, k6, k2tog, p2, k2tog, p2} rep. 144 sts.

Rnd 38: {K7, p2tog, p3, k7, p2, k1, p2} rep. 138 sts.

Rnd 39: {Ssk, k5, p1, p2tog, p1, k5, k2tog, p2, work inc 1-to-3, p2} rep. 132 sts.

Rnd 40: {K6, p1, p2tog, k6, p2, k3, p2} rep. 126 sts.

Rnd 41: {Ssk, k4, p2, k4, k2tog, p2, [k1, yo] twice, k1, p2} rep.

Rnd 42: Work even.

Rnd 43: {Ssk, k3, p2, k3, k2tog, p2, k2, yo, k1, yo, k2, p2} rep.

Rnd 44: Work even.

Rnd 45: {Ssk, k2, p2tog, k2, k2tog, p2, k3, yo, k1, yo, k3, p2} rep. 120 sts.

Rnd 46: Work even.

Rnd 47: {Ssk, k1, p1, k1, k2tog, p2, k7, k2tog, p2} rep. 102 sts.

Rnd 48: Work even.

Rnd 49: {Ssk, p1, k2tog, p2, k6, k2tog, p2} rep. 84 sts.

Rnd 50: {P3, p2tog, k7, p2tog} rep. 72 sts.

Rnd 51: Move marker one st to the right. P1, p2tog, p1, k5, k2tog, {p2, p2tog, p1, k5, k2tog} rep. 60 sts.

Rnd 52: {[P2tog] twice, k6} rep. 48 sts.

Rnd 53: {P2, k4, k2tog} rep. 42 sts.

Rnd 54: Work even.

Rnd 55: {P2, k3, k2tog} rep. 36 sts.

Rnd 56: Work even.

Rnd 57: {P2, k2, k2tog} rep. 30 sts.

Rnd 58: Work even.

Rnd 59: {P2tog, k1, k2tog} rep. 18 sts.

Rnd 60: {P1, k2tog} rep. 12 sts.

Rnd 61: K2tog 6 times. 6 sts.

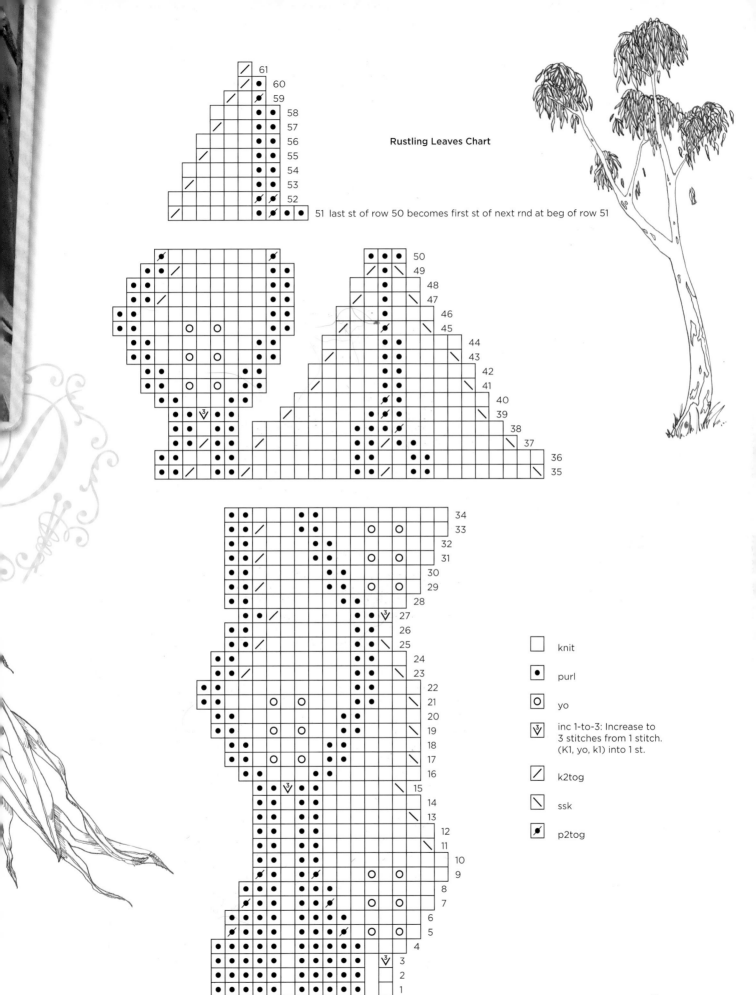

Rustling Leaves Chart

51 last st of row 50 becomes first st of next rnd at beg of row 51

	knit
•	purl
O	yo
⌄3	inc 1-to-3: Increase to 3 stitches from 1 stitch. (K1, yo, k1) into 1 st.
/	k2tog
\	ssk
∅	p2tog

At the east end of Portland, the Eastern Promenade wraps around the Munjoy Hill neighborhood. The Promenade's grassy hill slopes sharply downward to the ocean. From its paved walkways the "Prom", as locals call it, offers panoramic views of downtown, the harbor and Casco Bay. Although close to downtown, it's surprisingly quiet, with relatively little traffic. On sunny days the Prom is peppered with people reading, picnicking, or having some time with their thoughts.

Eastern Promenade

Munjoy Hill is where I officially fell in love with knitting. When Knitwit Yarn Shop opened its doors I found myself there most days. The neighborhood is home to many artists and shops, including Diane Toepfer's Ferdinand Home Store and Angela Adams, both of which have been inspirations to me. One of my favorite Portland restaurants is the contemporary Blue Spoon, found just a few blocks from the promenade. The owner, David, is a knitter himself!

The Eastern Promenade inspired the Panoramic Stole. With its sweeping shape and mesh lace pattern it's the perfect breezy companion for strolling along the path while taking in the amazing view.

PORTLAND, MAINE

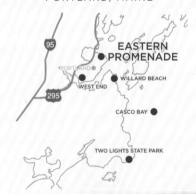

62

Walking paths that offer panoramic views of Casco Bay.

A wonderful organic
fingering weight yarn
created completely here
in Maine.

panoramic stole

A mesh lace stole that features just enough short row shaping to keep things interesting. Wonderfully long, this substantial extra layer can lend subtle drama to an outfit.

Shawl
CO 96 sts.

BEGIN PATTERNS
See next page for stitch patterns.

{Work rows 1-24 of Short Row Garter Stitch pattern. Work rows 1-4 of Mesh pattern 19 times.} Repeat these 2 sections 6 times total.

Work rows 1-24 of Short Row Garter Stitch pattern once more.

BO all sts.

Finishing
Weave in all ends on the WS. Wet block stole to measurements, following natural curve created by short rows.

Finished Measurements
Length: approx 80" / 203cm
Width: approx 19" / 49cm

Materials
2 skeins Swans Island *Fingering* (100% Organic Merino; 525 yds / 480m; 3½ oz / 100g) in Indigo OR 1000 yds / 915m of fingering weight yarn, such as The Fibre Company *Canopy Fingering* or Madelinetosh *Tosh Merino Light*.

US6 / 4mm 24" / 60cm or longer circular needle

Tapestry needle

Gauge
19½ sts and 33 rows = 4" / 10cm in Mesh pattern on US6 / 4mm needles or size needed to obtain gauge.

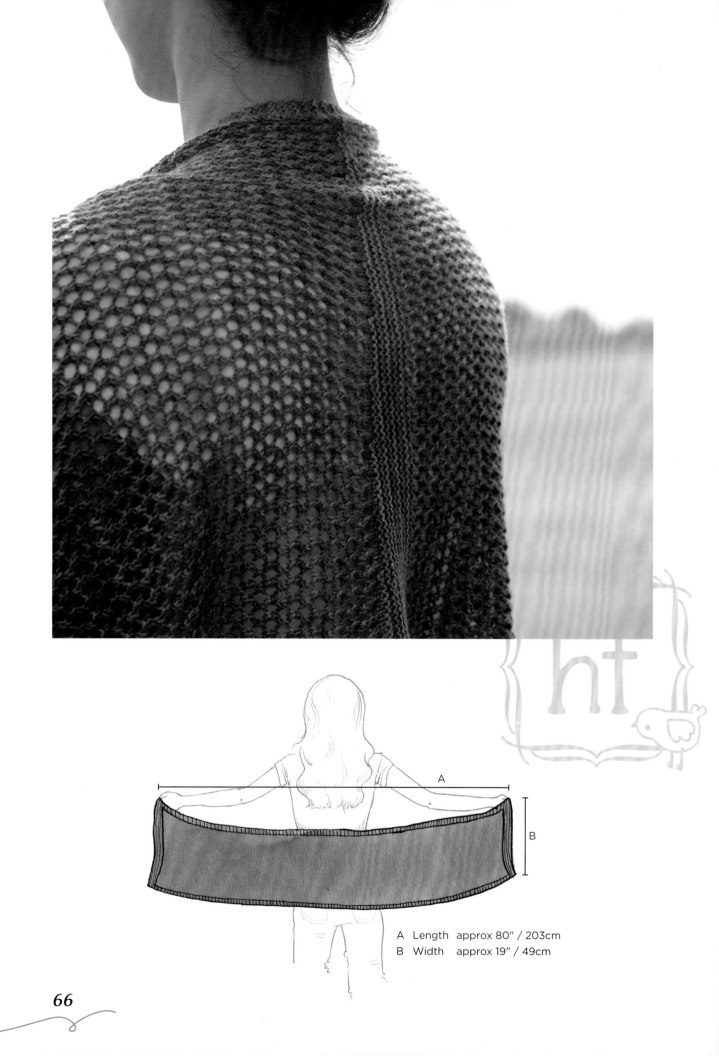

A Length approx 80" / 203cm
B Width approx 19" / 49cm

SHORT ROW GARTER STITCH PATTERN

Row 1: K8, w&t.

Row 2 and all WS rows: Knit.

Row 3: K16, w&t.

Row 5: K24, w&t.

Row 7: K32, w&t.

Row 9: K40, w&t.

Row 11: K48, w&t.

Row 13: K56, w&t.

Row 15: K64, w&t.

Row 17: K72, w&t.

Row 19: K80, w&t.

Row 21: K88, w&t.

Rows 23 and 24: Knit.

MESH PATTERN

Row 1 (RS): K4, {yo, k2tog} rep to last 4 sts, k4.

Row 2: K4, purl to last 4 sts, k4.

Row 3: K5, {ssk, yo} rep to last 5 sts, k5.

Row 4: K4, purl to last 4 sts, k4.

Cambria is a small town on the Central Coast known by the locals for being a perfect weekend getaway spot. Not only is the town itself charming with its quaint streets and locally owned shops, but it offers a spectacular beach experience as well. One of my all-time favorite places to visit in Cambria is Moonstone Beach. This beach is unlike any of the other beaches I've seen locally. The sand here at Moonstone is not your typical beach-sand. Instead, it is comprised of smooth colorful pebbles that shimmer in the sun. The pebbles come in a variety of shapes and sizes. I remember spending my time as a child carefully searching through the rocks trying to find the most interesting to add to my collection.

Moonstone Beach Boardwalk
CAMBRIA, CALIFORNIA

MOONSTONE BEACH
BOARDWALK

Moonstone Beach also features a raised wooden plank pathway known as "the Boardwalk". The path runs the entire length of the bluff with a gorgeous view of the shoreline. A colorful variety of local wildflowers and plant life line the walkway, with groupings of cypress trees providing a shady canopy overhead in many places. It is typical to see California ground squirrels peaking out from underneath the boardwalk and scurrying back and forth in front of you as you walk along. It is the perfect destination for a scenic stroll with your family.

The boardwalk overlooks beautiful Moonstone Beach. You can hear the waves crashing against the shore as you walk.

This section of the beach is often quite windy and the ocean air is always brisk. Many times I have found myself walking this path with my husband and daughter wishing I had brought a nice, thick scarf to wrap around me. This is what inspired me to create the **Cambrian Cowl** *knit from local Central Coast alpaca yarn. A cowl like this will keep you warm as you walk the Boardwalk and take in the amazing Cambrian sights.*

An incredibly soft and warm, locally-produced
alpaca yarn left in its natural color.

cambrian cowl

A quick-to-knit, bulky cowl that is both sophisticated and practical in its styling. The *Cambrian Cowl* can be worn buttoned up like a turtleneck for incredible warmth or left open as a stylish, folded down collar. The buttoned portion is knit in one piece, while the bottom section of the cowl is added later with picked up stitches. This is the perfect project to showcase a pair of very special buttons you have been saving.

Button Band

CO 20 sts. Do not join.

Ribbing setup row 1 (WS): {P1, k1} rep to last 2 sts, p2.

Mark the final st with a safety pin marker. This will mark the bottom edge of the cowl where you will be picking up sts later.

Ribbing setup row 2 (RS): K2, {p1, k1} rep.

Cont in est rib patt for 7 rows more. End on a WS row.

Setup row (RS): K18, p1, k1.
Next row (WS): P1, k1, p18.

Work even until work measures 20" / 50cm from CO edge. End on a WS row.

Buttonhole Band

Row 1 (RS): K2, {p1, k1} rep.
Row 2: {P1, k1} rep to last 2 sts, p2.
Rows 3 and 4: Rep rows 1 and 2 once more.
Row 5 (RS): Work 5 sts in patt, BO 3 sts, work 4 sts in patt, BO 3 sts, work remaining 3 sts in patt.
Row 6: Work across row in patt. Using backwards loop method, CO 3 sts over gaps.

Finished Measurements

Finished Measurements

Length: approx 8½" / 22cm
Circumference: approx 20" / 51cm around buttoned up section

Materials

2 skeins Alpenglow Yarn *Big Fat Alpaca* (100% Alpaca; 90 yds / 82m; 3½ oz / 100g), undyed OR approx 150 yds / 137m of bulky yarn, such as Misti Alpaca *Chunky.*

US10 / 6mm 16" / 40cm circular needle

Tapestry needle, safety pin to use as a marker, straight pins, 2 buttons 1½" / 4cm diameter, sewing needle and matching thread

Gauge

14 sts and 18 rows = 4" / 10cm in St st on US10 / 6mm needles or size needed to obtain gauge.

Row 7: K2, {p1, k1} rep.
Rows 8 and 9: Work even.

BO in rib.

Piece measures approx 22"/ 56cm from end to end. Wet block the piece at this stage to minimize rolling and help make picking up sts easier.

PICKING UP STITCHES

With WS facing, and the Buttonhole Band on the left hand side, fold both ends of rectangle in so that the Buttonhole Band is overlapping the Button Band completely. The Buttonhole Band will be visible, but the Button Band is hidden beneath. Using a couple of straight pins, pin the bands together to secure in place.

Using the safety pin marker as a guide, start at the end of the hidden Button Band on the bottom edge of the cowl and pick up and knit 68 sts around (about 3 sts for every 4 rows), picking up sts through both layers of overlapping fabric in the Button Band section. Pm, join to work in the rnd. Remove straight pins and safety pin marker.

Rnd 1 (RS): Knit.
Rnd 2: {K17, M1} rep. 72 sts.
Rnd 3: Knit.
Rnd 4: {K6, M1, k6} rep. 78 sts.

Rnds 5 and 6: Knit.
Rnd 7: {K13, M1} rep. 84 sts.

Work even in St st for 1" / 2.5cm.

Ribbing setup rnd: {K1, p1} rep.

Cont in est rib patt for 2 rnds more.

BO very loosely in rib.

Finishing

Weave in all ends on the WS. Wet block to measurements. Sew buttons onto Button Band opposite buttonholes.

A Circumference   20" / 51cm
B Length   8½" / 21.5cm

The West End

PORTLAND, MAINE

Of all the areas in Portland, the West End carries the most nostalgia for me. My husband and I lived most of our 10 "pre-children" years in this neighborhood. Downtown is just five minutes away, and yet it's so very quiet. Its wide, tree-lined streets feature amazing Victorian architecture. These streets inspired the **Branching Out Mitts.** *My husband and I often rode our bikes when we lived there, and these mitts would have been perfect on a cooler day.*

The Western Promenade is a grassy park that runs along the plateau that marks the edge of the West End. It offers a spectacular view of the highlands of western Maine and the White Mountains of New Hampshire. On a clear day you can see Mount Washington, which is 75 miles to the northwest. For four years we lived in the upstairs of an amazing house right on the promenade. We could climb up a set of narrow stairs to the widow's walk, and from there climb out a window to sit on the flat roof and enjoy the view from one of the highest points in Portland. It was especially fun to sit out there with friends at sunset and enjoy the view.

When morning sickness set in during my pregnancy, I would walk up and down these streets for hours, trying to distract myself. I'll always remember this time fondly, walking the pretty streets thinking about my baby. Though we now live a few miles away, we occasionally go back to walk as a family and reminisce about our years spent there.

A quiet neighborhood,
so close to downtown Portland.

this 100% baby alpaca yarn is very forgiving when knitting colorwork. I love the earthy colors!

branching out mitts

These little mitts knit up fast. They are worked flat and then seamed up one side. This is a great project for a few leftover skeins from your stash!

Right Mitt

With smaller straight needles and MC, CO 42 sts.

Ribbing setup row: {K1, p1} rep to end.

Cont in est rib patt for 1½" / 4cm from CO edge.

Switch to larger straight needles.

BEGIN WORKING CHART

Row 1 (RS): K1, pm, work row 1 of Right Mitt Chart over 20 sts, pm, k1, pm, knit to end.
Row 2: Purl to marker, sm, M1R, purl to marker, M1L, sm, work row 2 of Right Mitt Chart over 20 sts, sm, p1. 2 sts inc.
Row 3: K1, work chart, knit to end.
Row 4: Purl to 2nd marker, work chart, p1.
Row 5: K1, work chart, sm, M1L, knit to marker, M1R, sm, knit to end. 2 sts inc.
Row 6: Purl to 2nd marker, work chart, p1.
Row 7: K1, work chart, knit to end.

Rep rows 2-7 twice more, then rows 2-4 once more. 56 sts.

DIVIDE THUMB FROM MITT

Next row (RS): K1, work chart to marker, place 15 thumb sts on a holder, CO 1 st over gap, remove marker, knit to end. 42 sts.

Cont as est through row 41, working chart between markers.

With MC, purl 1 WS row.

Finished Measurements

Circumference: 7" / 17.5cm around widest part of hand

Materials

MC: 1 skein Blue Sky Alpacas *Melange* (100% Baby Alpaca; 110 yds / 100m; 1¾ oz / 50g) in Relish OR 110 yds / 101m of sport weight yarn such as Berroco *Ultra Alpaca Light*.

CC: 1 skein Blue Sky Alpacas *Melange* in Pumpernickel OR 40 yds / 37m of sport weight yarn such as Berroco *Ultra Alpaca Light*.

US5 / 3.75mm needles and dpns
US3 / 3.25mm needles and dpns

3 stitch markers, stitch holders, tapestry needle

Gauge

24 sts and 32 rows = 4" / 10cm in St st on US5 / 3.75mm needles or size needed to obtain gauge.

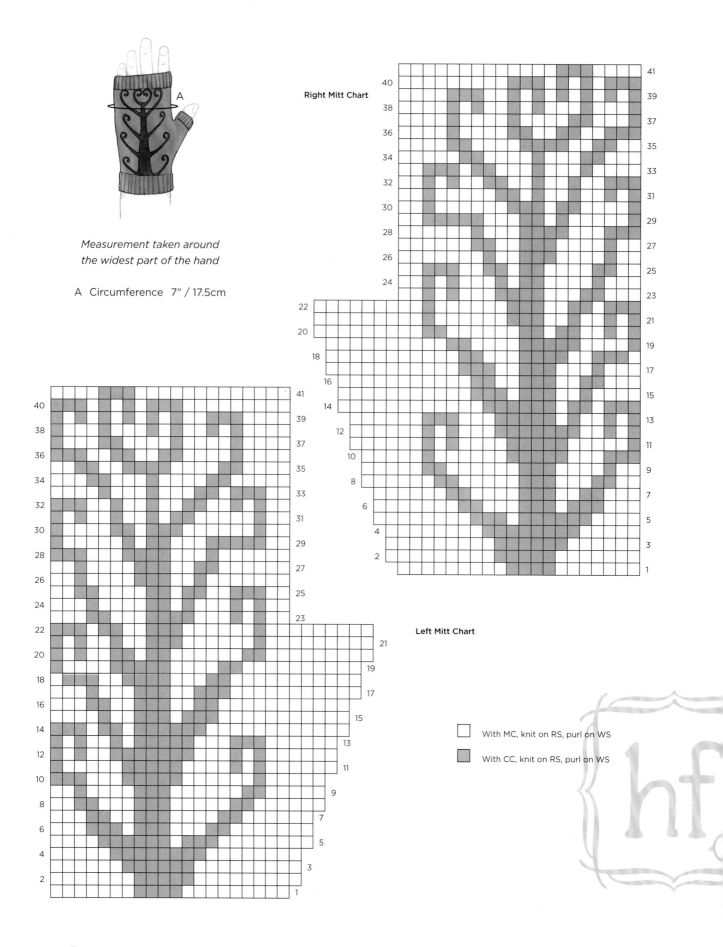

Measurement taken around
the widest part of the hand

A Circumference 7" / 17.5cm

Right Mitt Chart

Left Mitt Chart

☐ With MC, knit on RS, purl on WS

▨ With CC, knit on RS, purl on WS

78

Switch to smaller straight needles.

Ribbing setup row: {K1, p1} rep to end.

Cont in est rib patt for 4 rows more.

BO loosely in rib.

THUMB

Divide 15 held sts over 3 larger dpns as follows: 6 sts on 1st and 2nd needles, 3 sts on 3rd needle.

Next rnd: 1st and 2nd needles: with MC, knit; 3rd needle: k3, pick up and knit 1 st along the side of the thumb opening. Pm, join in the rnd. 16 sts.

Knit 4 rnds. Switch to smaller dpns.

Ribbing setup rnd: {K1, p1} rep to end.

Cont in est rib for 4 rnds more.

BO loosely in rib.

Left Mitt

With smaller straight needles and MC, CO 42 sts.

Ribbing setup row: {K1, p1} rep to end.

Cont in est rib patt for 1½" / 4cm from CO edge.

Switch to larger needles.

BEGIN WORKING CHART

Row 1 (RS): K20, pm, k1, pm, work row 1 of Left Mitt Chart over 20 sts, k1.
Row 2: P1, work row 2 of chart over 20 sts, sm, M1R, purl to marker, M1L, sm, purl to end. 2 sts inc.
Row 3: Knit to 2nd marker, work chart, k1.
Row 4: P1, work chart, purl to end.
Row 5: Knit to marker, sm, M1L, knit to marker, M1R, sm, work chart, k1. 2 sts inc.
Row 6: P1, work chart, purl to end.
Row 7: Knit to 2nd marker, work chart, k1.

Rep rows 2–7 twice more, then rows 2–4 once more. 56 sts.

DIVIDE THUMB FROM MITT

Knit to marker, remove marker, place 15 thumb sts on a holder, CO 1 st over gap, work chart, k1. 42 sts.

Cont as est through row 41, working chart between markers.

With MC, purl 1 WS row.

Switch to smaller straight needles.

Ribbing setup row: {K1, p1} rep to end.

Cont in est rib for 4 rnds more.

BO loosely in rib. Work Thumb as for Right Mitt.

Finishing

Seam outer edges together, forming a tube. Weave in all ends on the WS. Wet block to measurements.

Morro Strand Beach

Morro Bay is a local fishing town and harbor full of history. The bay was named after its famous landmark, Morro Rock, which is an extinct volcanic peak highly visible from all areas of town. This peak is part of the historic Nine Sisters, a grouping of ancient volcanos that run in a straight line for twelve miles.

In 1542, Portuguese navigator Juan Rodriguez Cabrillo named the rock El Morro, which in Spanish means "crown-shaped hill". Its regal presence gives character to the town and now serves as the protective home of the endangered Peregrine Falcon.

MORRO BAY, CALIFORNIA

MOONSTONE BEACH
BOARDWALK
101
ATASCADERO
MORRO STRAND
BEACH
SHELL CREEK ROAD
OAKS STATE RESERVE
SAN LUIS
OBISPO
MONTAÑA DE ORO
1

Morro Bay is our favorite place to go enjoy fish and chips by the ocean and, afterwards, to take a stroll downtown for some saltwater taffy. Many establishments offer dockside seating which allows you to look out into the harbor and watch the seagulls fly overhead and sea otters swim by.

Out of all of the beach spots in Morro Bay, the Morro Strand State Beach is our favorite. It is a beautifully clear stretch of beach with clean, light colored sand and a gorgeous view of the magnificent Morro Rock in the background. This stretch of shoreline is perfect for family outings and picnics. I am convinced that my 5-year old daughter would never tire of chasing the tide.

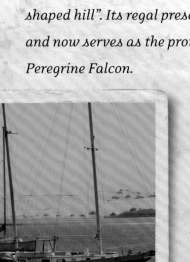

Fresh CRAB & SHRIMP COCKTAILS TO GO

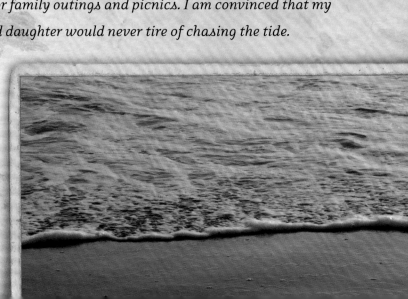

Watching the waves roll in is something that I have always found relaxing and enjoyable. I wanted to capture the look of the tide as it washes up on the Morro Strand shoreline in the **Sand and Sea Shawlette**. I am certainly glad to have historic and beautiful Morro Bay in such close proximity to us here on the Central Coast. I look forward to spending many more outings there with my growing family.

A view of Morro Rock from Morro Strand Beach.

A soothing combination of colors. The turquoise yarn has some seaweed content which I felt well represented this ocean-inspired design.

sand and sea shawlette

A light and lacy, crescent-shaped shawlette that drapes beautifully over your shoulders. *Sand and Sea* is knit from the top down in one piece. The curved shaping is created by the use of short rows.

Body

With MC, CO 253 sts. Do not join.

Knit 8 rows.

BEGIN SHORT ROW SHAPING

Short row 1 (RS): Knit until 6 sts rem, w&t.

Short row 2 (WS): Purl until 6 sts rem, w&t. 241 sts remain between wrapped sts.

Short row 3 (RS): Knit to 5 sts before last wrapped st, w&t.

Short row 4 (WS): Purl to 5 sts before last wrapped st, w&t.

Short rows 5–8: Rep last 2 rows twice more. 211 sts remain between wrapped sts.

Short row 9 (RS): Knit to 4 sts before last wrapped st, w&t.

Short row 10 (WS): Purl to 4 sts before last wrapped st, w&t.

Short rows 11–16: Rep last 2 rows 3 times more. 179 sts remain between wrapped sts.

Short row 17 (RS): Knit to 3 sts before last wrapped st, w&t.

Short row 18 (WS): Purl to 3 sts before last wrapped st, w&t.

Short rows 19–28: Rep last 2 rows 5 times more. 143 sts remain between wrapped sts.

Finished Measurements
Length: approx 48" / 122cm from end to end
Width: approx 12" / 31cm at widest point of center, including border

Materials
MC: 1 skein Madelinetosh *Prairie* (100% Merino Wool; 840 yds / 768m; 4 oz / 114g) in Vintage Frame OR approx 250 yds / 225m of lace weight yarn, such as Malabrigo *Lace*.

CC: 1 skein Handmaiden *Sea Silk* (70% Silk, 30% Seacell; 437 yds / 400m; 3½ oz / 100g) in Peridot OR approx 125 yds / 115m of fingering weight yarn, such as Malabrigo *Sock* or Madelinetosh *Tosh Sock*.

US6 / 4mm 32" / 40cm circular needle

Tapestry needle

Gauge
24 sts and 36 rows = 4" / 10cm in St st on US6 / 4mm needles or size needed to obtain gauge.

Short row 29 (RS): Knit to 2 sts before last wrapped st, w&t.

Short row 30 (WS): Purl to 2 sts before last wrapped st, w&t.

Short rows 31–52: Rep last 2 rows 11 times more. 95 sts remain between wrapped sts.

Short row 53 (RS): Knit to 1 st before last wrapped st, w&t.

Short row 54 (WS): Purl to 1 st before last wrapped st, w&t.

Short rows 55 and 56: Rep last 2 rows once more. 91 sts remain between wrapped sts.

Short row 57 (RS): Knit to 3 sts before last wrapped st, w&t.

Short row 58 (WS): Purl to 3 sts before last wrapped st, w&t.

Short rows 59–70: Rep last 2 rows 6 times more. 49 sts remain between wrapped sts.

Short row 71 (RS): Knit to 5 sts before last wrapped st, w&t.

Short row 72 (WS): Purl to 5 sts before last wrapped st, w&t. 39 sts remain between wrapped sts.

Row 73 (RS): Knit, picking up and knitting wraps as you go.

Row 74 (WS): Purl, picking up and purling remaining wraps as you go.

Increase row (RS): {Kfb, k1} across row, until there is 1 st remaining, kfb. 380 sts.

Feather and Fan Edging
Switch to CC.

Rows 1 and 2: Knit.
Row 3 (WS): Purl.
Row 4 (RS): K1, (k2tog) 3 times, (yo, k1) 6 times, *(k2tog) 6 times, (yo, k1) 6 times; rep from * until 7 sts remain, (k2tog) 3 times, k1.
Rows 5 and 6: Knit.
Row 7: Purl.

Rep rows 4–7 once more.

Next row (RS): K1, (k2tog) 3 times, (yo, k1) 6 times, yo, *(k2tog) 6 times, (yo, k1) 6 times, yo; rep from * until 7 sts remain, (k2tog) 3 times, k1. 401 sts.
Next row: Knit.

BO all sts purlwise very loosely.

Finishing
Weave in all ends on WS. Wet block to measurements.

NOTE: Blocking is crucial to the shawl draping well and the edging lying flat.

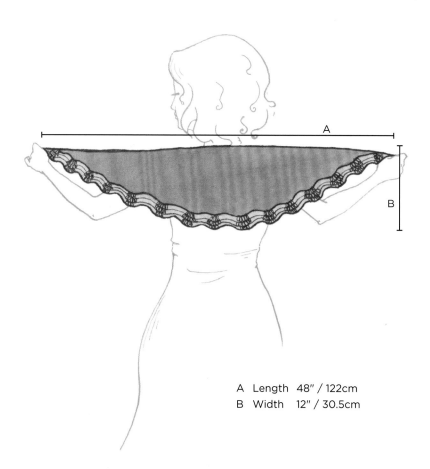

A Length 48″ / 122cm
B Width 12″ / 30.5cm

Garter stitch

Knit all rows when working flat. Alternate knit 1 round, purl 1 round when working in the round.

I-cord

When working I-cord, work is not turned. * Using a double-pointed needle, knit one row. Instead of turning the work around to work back on the wrong side, slide all stitches to the other end of the needle, switch the needle back to your left hand, bring the yarn around the back of the work, and knit across again, giving the yarn a sharp tug after 2 stitches to close the gap. Repeat from * to form I-cord. After a few rows, the work will begin to form a tube.

Kitchener stitch

Also known as grafting. For complete instructions please visit: http://knitty.com/ISSUEsummer04/FEATtheresasum04.html

M1 Increases

M1(L): MAKE 1 (LEFT) INCREASE

Lift bar between stitches from front to back with the left needle and then knit through the back of it with the right needle.

M1R: MAKE 1 RIGHT INCREASE

Lift bar between stitches from back to front with the left needle and then knit through the front of it with the right needle.

Short rows

WRAP AND TURN

Right Side (RS): Work in pattern to the stitch to be wrapped, move yarn to front of work and slip next stitch as if to knit. Bring yarn to back and turn work to other side. With WS facing, slip same stitch back to right needle as if to purl. Proceed to work across row in pattern.
Wrong Side (WS): Work in pattern to the stitch to be wrapped, move yarn to back of work and slip next stitch as if to purl. Bring yarn to front and turn work to other side. With RS facing, slip same stitch back to right needle as if to purl. Proceed to work across row in pattern.

The resulting wrap will look like a "necklace" or "noose" around your stitch.

PICKING UP WRAPS

NOTE: Picking up and knitting the wraps, while not absolutely necessary, makes the wraps invisible and produces a much neater look to your finished piece.

Pull each wrap over to the wrong side of your work as follows:

Right Side (RS): Work to previously wrapped stitch. Insert right needle tip under wrap from the bottom up. Pull it up and over the stitch it was wrapping and onto the needle. The wrap will now be behind the stitch on the left needle. Knit both the stitch and the wrap together through the back loop. The wrap should be completely invisible from the RS.
Wrong Side (WS): Work to previously wrapped stitch. Insert right hand needle tip under wrap on the RS of your work from the bottom up (just as for the RS instructions). Since the WS is facing you, you will have to twist your work to do this. Pull it up and over the stitch it was wrapping towards the WS that is facing you and onto the needle. The wrap will now be behind the stitch on the left hand needle. Purl both the stitch and the wrap together. The wrap should be completely invisible from the RS.

Stockinette stitch

Knit on the right side, purl on the wrong side when working flat. Knit all rounds when working in the round.

Work even

Work stitches in pattern as they appear without increasing or decreasing.

ABBREVIATIONS

approx: approximately

beg: begin(s)(ning)

BO: Bind Off (Cast Off)

CC: Contrasting Color

circ: circumference

cn: cable needle

CO: Cast On

cont: continue(s)(ing)

dec: decrease(s)(d)(ing)

dpn(s): double-pointed needle(s)

est: establish(ed)

inc: increase(s)(d)(ing)

k: knit

k2tog: knit 2 stitches together

kfb: knit into front and back of stitch

MC: Main Color

p: purl

p2tog: purl 2 stitches together

patt(s): pattern(s)

pfb: purl into front and back of stitch

pm: place marker

rep(s): repeat(s)

rnd(s): round(s)

RS: Right Side

s2kp2: Slip 2 stitches together to the right needle as if to knit, knit the next stitch, then pass the 2 slipped stitches over.

sl: slip

sm: slip marker

ssk: slip, slip, knit. Slip 2 stitches individually to the right needle as if to knit, then slide the left needle into the stitches from left to right and knit the 2 stitches together.

st(s): stitch(es)

St st: Stockinette stitch (see Techniques)

tbl: through back of loop(s)

w&t: wrap and turn (see Techniques)

WS: Wrong Side

yo: yarn over

RESOURCES

Alpenglow Yarn
www.alpenglowyarn.com

Blue Sky Alpacas
PO Box 88
Cedar, MN 55011
888.460.8862
www.blueskyalpacas.com

Handmaiden Fine Yarn
www.handmaiden.ca

Kelbourne Woolens
(Distributor for The Fibre Company)
2000 Manor Road
Conshohocken, PA 19428
215.687.5534
www.kelbournewoolens.com

Madelinetosh
7515 Benbrook Parkway
Benbrook, TX 76126
877.546.3066
www.madelinetosh.com

Pigeonroof Studios
pigeonroofstudios.etsy.com

Quince & Company
info@quinceandco.com
www.quinceandco.com

String Theory Hand Dyed Yarn
132 Beech Hill Road
Blue Hill, Maine 04614
207.374.9990
www.stringtheoryyarn.com

Swans Island
231 Atlantic Highway (Route 1)
Northport, ME 04849
888.526.9526
www.swansislandblankets.com

Tactile Fiber Arts
510.932.2768
www.tactilefiberarts.com

Tangled Yarns
www.tangledyarns.com.au
(Cambrian Cowl buttons on pages 68–73)

Wooden Treasures
woodentreasures.etsy.com
(Gnarled Oak buttons on pages 26–33)

ACKNOWLEDGMENTS

A special thank you to our hero and graphic designer, **Mary Joy Gumayagay**. You turned our ideas for a book into a reality and without you, *Coastal Knits* wouldn't be what it is. Thank you for elevating our collection to unbelievable heights!

Thanks to **Tana Pageler** for all your hard work as our technical editor, and for the assistance of **Cecily Glowik MacDonald** and **Kristen TenDyke**.

Thank you to **Carrie Hoge** for your beautiful photography of the East Coast designs, and to **Hunter Johnson** and **Scott Enos** for your photography assistance on the West Coast.

Thank you to **Neesha Hudson** for your unique coastal illustrations. They greatly add to the presentation of this book.

Thank you to our beautiful models **Andrea Harrington** and **Jocelyn Miller** for patiently enduring photo shoots in the middle of summer.

Thank you to **Alpenglow Yarn, Blue Sky Alpacas, Kelbourne Woolens, Madelinetosh, Pigeonroof Studios, Quince & Company, String Theory Hand Dyed Yarn, Swans Island** and **Tactile Fiber Arts** for providing your amazing yarns for use in our designs.

And thanks to our fabulous test knitters, **Andrea Sanchez, Anne Ginger, Ariane Caron-Lacoste, Deirdre Kennedy, Eliana Bahri, Erica Dakos, Nicole Dupuis, Peter Kennedy, Sarah Cote** and **Veronika Jobe** for all of your help in making these patterns just right for our readers.

Everyone involved helped to shape *Coastal Knits* into something that we are truly proud of.

We couldn't have done it without you!